Routledge Revision

Business Law

2012–2013

Routledge Q&A s

Each Routledge Q&

found on exam pa

written by lecturer

insight into exactly

excellent revision a

Q&As sold to date,

New editions publi

Business Law

Intellectual Propert

Published in 2011:

Civil Liberties & Hu

Commercial Law

Company Law

Constitutional & A

Contract Law

Criminal Law

For a full listing, vis

Routledge Revision: Questions & Answers

Business Law

2012–2013

Janice Denoncourt

Senior Lecturer at Nottingham Trent University

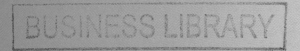

 Routledge
Taylor & Francis Group

LONDON AND NEW YORK

Second edition published 2012
by Routledge
2 Park Square, Milton Park, Abingdon, Oxon, OX14 4RN

Simultaneously published in the USA and Canada
by Routledge
711 Third Avenue, New York, NY 10017

Routledge is an imprint of the Taylor & Francis Group, an informa business

Previous editions published by Routledge
First edition   2010

British Library Cataloguing in Publication Data
A catalogue record for this book is available from the British Library

ISBN: 978–0–415–68842–0 (pbk)
ISBN: 978–0–203–12745–2 (ebk)

Typeset in TheSans
by RefineCatch Limited, Bungay, Suffolk

1006894343

MIX
Paper from
responsible sources
FSC
www.fsc.org   FSC® C004839

Printed and bound in Great Britain by
TJ International Ltd, Padstow, Cornwall

Contents

Preface

This is the second edition of *Q&A Business Law* in the Routledge Revision: Questions & Answers series. The aim of the text is to assist business law students prepare for and succeed in their exams. A series of 53 problem, essay, short answer and multiple-choice questions has been topically arranged followed by an answer plan and a suggested answer.

Business law evolves from its environment; therefore, the content of this text reflects the latest trends in business law. Traditional areas of law as well as contemporary topics such as e-commerce, intellectual property rights, advertising law and environmental law are covered. Recent attention on corporate scandals has led to a greater focus on professional values, ethics and governance – especially as law reform moves towards strengthening codes of conduct, regulation and legislation. Where possible, current social, ethical and international issues are included in the material. In addition, there is advice on business law exam technique and a list of weblinks to provide extra resources for students who want to take their exam preparation further.

Q&A Business Law is a study aid appropriate for the following:

(a) undergraduate business law and civil obligations courses;
(b) graduate introduction to business law courses, especially MBA courses;
(c) entrepreneurship courses with a business law module;
(d) law access courses;
(e) small business people or evening business law classes.

Once again, I also wish to express my thanks to many special people:

To the lecturers and professors at Curtin University in Perth, Western Australia who gave me my first exposure to the 'Law'.

To Fiona Kinnear, Commissioning Editor and Damian Mitchell, Editorial Assistant, for their assistance to produce the second edition of *Q&A Business Law*.

To my mentor and colleague, Graham Ferris (Reader in Law at Nottingham Trent).

Business law is an incredibly popular subject in business schools, despite its reputation for being a tough course. This is because it introduces business students to legal issues that will affect them in their future commercial endeavours. Students also learn a little about the legal profession, their professional cousins, with whom many will interact closely over the course of their careers.

Those who really enjoy studying business law have been known to pursue a law degree and a career in law – exactly what I did! After I qualified, I went to work for a large commercial law firm and then as in-house counsel for a publicly listed company. As a result of my professional legal experience I espouse the following statement, which I hope all business students will sear into their memories:

> Discourage litigation. Persuade your neighbours to compromise whenever you can. Point out to them how the nominal winner is often the real loser – in fees, expenses, and waste of time. As a peace-maker, the lawyer has a superior opportunity of being a good man. There will be business enough.
>
> Abraham Lincoln

I have attempted to state the law as it stands on 31 July 2011. I apologise if inadvertently any sources remain unacknowledged and will be glad to make the necessary arrangements at the earliest opportunity.

Janice Denoncourt
Senior Lecturer in Law
Nottingham Trent University
31 July 2011

Law Report Abbreviations

The following list sets out the abbreviations used when citing law reports.

AC	Law Reports, Appeal Cases
All ER	All England Law Reports
All ER (Comm)	All England Law Reports (Commercial Cases)
All ER (EC)	All England Law Reports (European Cases)
All ER Rep	All England Law Reports Reprint
App Cas	Law Reports, Appeal Cases
ATC	Annotated Tax Cases
BCC	British Company Law and Practice
BCLC	Butterworths Company Law Cases
B & CR	Reports of Bankruptcy and Companies Winding-up Cases
Ch	Law Reports, Chancery Division
Cl & Fin	Clark & Finnelly's Reports
CLY	Current Law Yearbook
CMLR	Common Market Law Reports
Co Rep	Coke's Reports (1572–1616)
Com Case	Commercial Cases
EHRR	European Human Rights Reports
EWCA Civ	England and Wales Court of Appeal Civil Division
Fam	Law Report, Family Division
HL	House of Lords
ICR	Industrial Court Reports
IRLB	Industrial Relations Law Bulletin
IRLR	Industrial Relations Law Reports
ITR	Reports of decision of the Industrial Tribunals
KB	Law Reports, King's Bench Division
L & TR	Landlord and Tenant Reports
LGR	Local Government Reports
Lloyd LR or Lloyd's Rep	Lloyd's List Law Reports
LRQB	Law Reports, Queen's Bench
LRRP	Law Reports Restrictive Practices
M & W	Messon & Welsby's Reports (1837–1847)
NLJ	New Law Journal

P	Law Reports, Probate, Divorce and Admiralty Division
P & CR	Planning and Compensation Reports 1949 – current
PIQR	Personal Injuries and Quantum Reports
QB	Law Reports Queen's Bench Division
Sol Jo	Solicitors' Journal
STC	Simon's Tax Cases
Tax Cas or TC	Tax Cases 1875 – current
TLR	Times Law Reports
WLR	Weekly Law Reports

How to Study Business Law

At first, many business students are overwhelmed by the study of law, which is so different from studying accounting, marketing, economics, human resources or information technology. They are alienated by what at first seems like an arcane body of knowledge, expressed in formal legal language ('legalese'), rather than in plain English. Learning the law is like learning a foreign language! Understanding the legal terminology is the starting point.

A business law student should approach business law study by learning:

1. the relevant legal terminology;
2. the framework of the particular area of law, for example relevant legislation;
3. the details of the law, namely the leading cases (precedents), especially judgments made by the Law Lords in the Supreme Court (formerly the House of Lords);
4. to apply the law to a set of facts or problem in writing.

For example, when beginning to study company law, the student should generally familiarise her/himself with the relevant provisions of the **Companies Act 2006** and then learn the leading case law, for example *Salomon v Salomon & Co* (1897) House of Lords; *Macaura v Northern Assurance Ltd* (1925) House of Lords.

It is a misconception to think that studying law is dull and merely a matter of memorising cases and reproducing them. There is little to be gained by merely rote learning the legislation and case law if you cannot apply it. As the old saying goes: 'One pound of learning requires ten pounds of common sense to apply it.'

Typical legal problem questions set out the facts and then require you to advise the parties by putting yourself in the position of the judge. The judge has to apply the precedent case law to the facts at hand, distinguishing the facts when necessary in order to arrive at an outcome. The more key cases you know, understand and can quote to support your arguments, the better you will understand the subject and the better your assessment performance will be. Yes, you have to learn and know cases, but the true attraction of studying law lies in the variety of ways the legal principles might apply to any given situation.

LexisNexis and Westlaw are the primary electronic databases for accessing case law. These databases contain summaries of most cases and full-text versions of many of them. Access the database from your university's library law web pages.

The above process will get you through your course and *Q&A* will help you to apply and review your newly acquired knowledge in order to succeed in your assessment.

Once you get past the legalese, what you are doing is basically high-level research. It may motivate your study to remember that the knowledge of the law you develop will help you to wield more power than most people and to make more money than your competitors!

MORE PRACTICAL STUDY TIPS

❖ Ensure you understand perfectly from your lecturer exactly how you will be assessed.
❖ At the beginning of the course ask about whether the assessment will include essay, problem, short answer or multiple-choice questions.
❖ Ask which materials you will be allowed to have access to during the assessment; for example will you be able to refer to an un-annotated copy of the relevant legislation; or is it an 'open book' exam or a 'closed book' exam?
❖ Usually, the lecturer and course tutors are involved in setting and marking the assessments. Take note of the hints they give about important areas of the law during the lectures and tutorials. It is quite likely that they offer this information to help those who diligently attend class to prepare well for the assessment.

Table of Cases

Table of Legislation

STATUTES

SECONDARY LEGISLATION

INTERNATIONAL LEGISLATION

Guide to the Companion Website

http://www.routledge.com/textbooks/revision

Visit the Routledge Q&A website to discover even more study tips and advice on getting those top marks.

On the Routledge revision website you'll find the following resources designed to enhance your revision on all areas of undergraduate law.

The Good, The Fair, & The Ugly

Good essays are the gateway to top marks. New to this edition, this interactive tutorial provides sample essays together with voice-over commentary and tips for successful exam essays, written by our Q&A authors themselves.

Multiple Choice Questions

Knowledge is the foundation of every good essay. Focusing on key examination themes, these MCQs have been written to test your knowledge and understanding of each subject in the book.

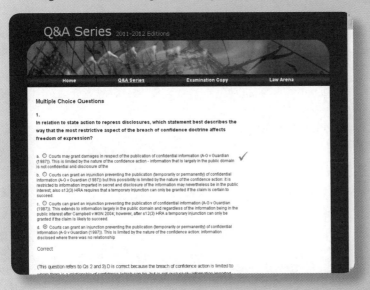

Bonus Q&As

Having studied our exam advice, put your revision into practice and test your essay-writing skills with our additional online questions and answers.

Don't forget to check out even more revision guides and exam tools from Routledge!

Lawcards

Lawcards are your complete, pocket-sized guides to key examinable areas of the undergraduate law.

Routledge Student Statutes

Comprehensive selections; clear, easy to use layout; alphabetical, chronological, and thematic indexes; and a competitive price make *Routledge Student Statutes* the statute book of choice for the serious law student.

Introduction

Legal education no longer exists exclusively for law students who wish to enter the legal profession. Increasingly, law components are found in many other degree programmes, especially in business schools. In addition, inclusion of such modules is very often an accreditation requirement set by professional bodies.

However, business law modules do not try to teach business students to be lawyers. These courses can only provide a brief introduction to key legal topics. The aim is to show students how the law works and affects business operations. Knowledge of the law will assist future business people with their decision-making and ethics and, hopefully, help them to develop an awareness of when they need to seek legal advice.

Typically, business law students are introduced to the main themes and concepts of English law and the English legal system with a focus on particular legal topics relevant to business schools. Topics generally include the principles of contract, tort, partnership, company, employment and intellectual property law, among others. The legal principles are placed in the context of the legal system, the courts and business transactions. This foundation knowledge of law is so important! One of the things I've learned over years working for and within businesses is that people who know how the law affects their business run the most successful businesses.

Business law courses are usually taught by academic lawyers from the law school who provide 'service teaching' to the business school. Right away, business students are introduced to a lecturer (a professional from another tribe!) who thinks like a lawyer and adopts a critical legal analysis approach that is foreign to them. Students will quickly have to grasp how to study law if they are to succeed with their law studies. The modules often work as follows:

❖ Students will generally receive two to three hours of lectures per week. The lecture is essentially a guide to the conceptual framework for further reading of the relevant textbook chapter or journal article.

- ❖ Students will then have an opportunity to apply the law via a series of tutorial questions or seminar discussions. These sessions provide the interactive dimension and students are expected to be prepared in order to effectively participate.
- ❖ Often times, a piece of coursework such as an essay must be submitted.
- ❖ Usually, there is a final written exam.

In the context of business studies, the crucial ingredient of a legal education is how to identify and analyse legal issues in order to give appropriate advice after considering both sides of the argument. The law is constantly changing and therefore proposed changes need to be debated and discussed. Adopting this approach will assist students to appreciate the different layers of the law that apply to business and to recognise the impact that changes in legislation and new case law may have on a given industry.

Introduction to the English Legal System and the Courts

INTRODUCTION

What is law? Every society makes and enforces laws that govern the conduct of individuals, businesses and other organisations that function within it.

Businesses that are established in the United Kingdom are subject to UK law. They are also subject to the laws of other countries in which they operate. Businesses of other countries must adhere to UK law when doing business here. The laws of business exist to protect persons (including legal persons such as companies) as well as the public. These laws must be obeyed and followed, otherwise there will be legal consequences, for example fines or imprisonment.

By world standards, UK law is generally regarded as one of the most comprehensive, fair, democratic and effective systems of law ever developed and enforced, particularly with respect to commerce. UK law evolves and changes along with the norms of society, developments in technology and the growth and expansion of commerce in the UK and in the world.

The philosophy of the law is referred to as jurisprudence. There are several different philosophies about how the law developed including:

School of thought	Idea
Natural law	The law is based on what is morally correct and ethical.
Historical	The law consists of social traditions and customs.
Analytical	The law is shaped by logic.
Sociological	The law provides a way to advance certain goals in the best interests of society.
Command	The law is the set of rules created and enforced by the governing party.
Critical legal studies	Legal rules are unnecessary and legal disputes should be solved by using rules based on fairness.

Law and economics   Promoting market efficiency should be the key
                            concern of the law.

Before the Norman Conquest in 1066, each locality in England was subject to local laws established by the local ruling lord or chieftain. After 1066, William the Conqueror and his successors to the throne of England began to replace the local laws with one uniform system of law. English common law was developed over centuries by judges appointed by the king or queen, who delivered their opinions when deciding particular cases brought to court. At the time, the law emphasised legal procedure for bringing a case to court over the merit of the case. The only remedy available in the law courts was a monetary award of damages (compensation).

Given the unfair judgments and limited remedies available in the law courts, the Court of Chancery (or equity) was established under the authority of the Lord Chancellor. People who believed the law courts' decisions were unfair could appeal to the Court of Chancery for an appropriate remedy and this Court would consider the merits of the case. The Chancellor's remedies were called equitable remedies, because they were designed to deal with particular fact situations. Equitable orders took precedence over the legal decisions and remedies of the law courts. An Act of Parliament merged the two court systems in the nineteenth century and so now a person can seek justice in just one court system.

SOURCES OF LAW IN THE UK

There is no single set of written rules that make up 'the law'. Instead there are seven different sources of law that interact with each other. These sources of law are:

❖ Statute – passed by Parliament;
❖ Delegated legislation – statutory instruments drawn up by government departments, bylaws made by local authorities, and orders in council are regulations made by the government at a time of national emergency (such as in wartime);
❖ Case law – also known as the 'common law', made by the decisions of judges in individual cases which reach the higher courts;
❖ European Union (EU) Law – incorporates the **European Convention on Human Rights** into English law in the **Human Rights Act 1988**. On questions of EU law, the European Court of Justice binds all the other UK courts;
❖ International treaties – may incorporate their provisions directly into UK law;
❖ Custom – is traditional local commercial practice, but it arises seldom except in shipping law;
❖ Equity – is historical, derived from the law of the King or his Chancellor's conscience as a Christian, especially to fill perceived gaps in the common law.

DOCTRINE OF *STARE DECISIS* (LATIN FOR 'TO STAND BY THE DECISION')

This doctrine holds that past court decisions become a binding precedent for deciding future cases. In other words, lower courts must follow the precedent established by higher courts. That is why the lower courts must follow all House of Lords decisions in the English legal system.

CRITICAL LEGAL THINKING

Judges apply legal reasoning to reach their decision in a particular case. This means that the judge must specify the issue(s) in the case, identify the relevant facts and then apply the law to the facts to conclude the issue presented. This process is called critical legal thinking.

KEY TERMS

- ❖ Claimant – the party who brings the case to court;
- ❖ Defendant – the party who must answer the case;
- ❖ Appellant – the party who appealed the decision of the trial court or court of first instance. An appellant may be either the claimant or the respondent depending on who lost the case at trial or lower court level;
- ❖ Respondent – the party who must answer the appellant's appeal. The respondent may be either the claimant or the defendant, depending on which party appeals.

WRITING A CASE BRIEF

The best way to study a case is to follow the procedure set out below:

1. The case name, citation and court;
2. A summary of the relevant facts in the case;
3. The issue of the case stated as a one-sentence question answerable only by yes or no;
4. A summary of the court's reasoning for their decision (*ratio decidendi*).

TYPES OF LAW

There are many different areas of law, but the most important divisions are between:

- ❖ criminal and civil law; and
- ❖ public and private law.

'Criminal law' deals with wrongs that are considered so serious as to be an offence against the whole community. For this reason, they are prosecuted in the name of the state (or specifically the Queen, e.g. *R v Brown*). It is also possible to bring a private prosecution, but this happens relatively rarely. In criminal cases there is a public prosecutor who prosecutes a defendant in the criminal courts. The allegations of criminal conduct must be proved beyond a reasonable doubt. If the prosecution is successful, the defendant is found guilty (convicted) and may be punished by the courts. If the prosecution is unsuccessful, the defendant is found not guilty and acquitted.

'Civil law' covers everything else, from road traffic matters and injured parties suing for compensation or neighbours fighting over who owns a fence, to magazines being sued for libel and businesses disputing a tax ruling by the Inland Revenue. Civil law is concerned with the rights and duties that arise between individuals. In civil proceedings a claimant sues a defendant in the civil courts. The claimant will be successful if s/he can prove her/his case on the balance of probabilities, that is, the evidence weighs more in favour of the claimant than of the defendant. If the claimant's civil action is successful, the defendant will be held liable and the court will order an appropriate remedy, usually damages (financial compensation).

Both 'public' and 'private' law are aspects of civil law. Private law comprises disputes between individual parties, such as someone injured in an accident suing the person who caused it, or a celebrity suing a newspaper for libel. Public law is the set of legal principles that govern the way the public authorities, including the government, use their powers. Public authorities cannot act as they please, but can only exercise the powers given to them by law. Public law sets out the framework for the exercise of such powers to ensure that the powers are not exceeded or misused. The main form of action in public law is the application for judicial review. This allows individuals (or organisations) to challenge the decisions or acts of public bodies.

QUESTION 1 --

What is law, why is it important for society and what is its function? Do you favour any particular legal school of thought?

Answer Plan

This essay question has four parts that the student must answer:

(1) What is law?
Refer to the main sources of English law.

(2) Why is law important for society?

It is a set of rules to regulate conduct, and protect persons and their property.

(3)   What is the function of the law?
Keeping the peace, shaping moral standards, promoting social justice, maintaining the status quo, facilitating orderly change and planning and maximising individual freedoms.

(4)   Do you favour any particular legal school of thought?
Note the various schools of legal jurisprudence, for example natural, historical, analytical, sociological, law and economics, and decide which jurisprudence you prefer and why.

ANSWER

Every society makes and enforces laws that govern the conduct of the individuals, businesses and other organisations (e.g. government, charities) that function within it. Although UK law is primarily based on English common law, EU law and international treaties also influence it. The sources of law in England and Wales include the following:

❖ Statutes passed by Parliament;
❖ Delegated legislation (statutory instruments drawn up by government departments, bylaws made by local authorities, and Orders in Council which are regulations made by the government at a time of national emergency (such as in wartime);
❖ Case law, also known as the 'common law', made by the decisions of judges in individual cases which reach the higher courts;
❖ European Union (EU) law incorporates the **European Convention on Human Rights** into English law in the **Human Rights Act 1988**. On questions of EU law, the European Court of Justice (ECJ) binds all the other UK courts;
❖ International treaties may incorporate their provisions directly into UK law;
❖ Custom is traditional local commercial practice, but it arises seldom, except in shipping law;
❖ Equity is historical, derived from the law of the King or his Chancellor's conscience as a Christian, especially to fill perceived gaps in the common law.

What is the law and why is it important for society? The law consists of rules that regulate conduct of persons, including legal persons such as companies. It is intended to protect persons and their property against unwanted interference from others. In other words, the law forbids persons to engage in certain undesirable activities.

The concept of 'law' is broad. Although it is difficult to define with precision, *Black's Law Dictionary* states that: 'Law, in its generic sense, is a body of rules of action or conduct prescribed by controlling authority, and having binding legal force. That which must be obeyed and followed by citizens subject to sanctions or legal consequences is a law.' In England, the law has several functions. At the most basic level, the law functions to keep the peace (e.g. enacting laws to prevent fraud). The law shapes moral standards (e.g. enacting laws to discourage or prohibit stealing or driving while under the influence of alcohol) and promotes social justice by, for example, laws that prohibit sex discrimination in employment. The law also facilitates the organisation of society by maintaining the status quo, for example to prevent the unlawful overthrow of a lawfully elected government and to facilitate change by only passing legislation after considerable debate in Parliament. Helping society to plan for the future is another example of the function of the law, for example by the enactment of environmental laws to minimise pollution. One of the most important recent functions of the law is to maximise human rights, such as the right to a fair trial, freedom of religion and association, among others.

Legal and political philosophers have often debated how the law should develop and several jurisprudential schools of thought have evolved as a result of scholarship. Classical legal philosophies can be grouped into several schools, known as the Natural Law School, the Historical Law School, the Analytical School, the Sociological School, the Critical Legal Studies School and the Law and Economics School. As a future member of the business community, the latter modern school of jurisprudential thought is to be preferred. The Law and Economics School seeks to promote market efficiency and argues that this should be the central goal of legal decision-making, especially in connection with laws that affect business, such as company and insolvency laws.

As stated by the eminent Roscoe Pound in his 1923 text, *Interpretations of Legal History*: 'Law must be stable and yet it cannot stand still.' It is important to recognise that English law evolves and changes along with the norms of society, technology and the growth and expansion of commerce in England and around the world. As a result of the development of the law over hundreds of years, the English legal system in England and Wales is one of the most comprehensive, fair and democratic systems ever developed and enforced.

Common Pitfalls ✗

This is a four-part question and calls for effective time management to deal with each part relatively equally.

QUESTION 2

Explain why the law of equity developed and how it was an advance on the common
law system of justice. What is the present relationship between the two systems?

Answer Plan

This is a typical essay question that requires the student to discuss the role of
equity in the English legal system.

- ❖   Define and explain the term 'equity';
- ❖   Outline how a second set of courts known as Chancery or Equity courts
  developed, why they were needed and why they were an improvement on
  the common law system of justice;
- ❖   Illustrate the new rules by setting out the maxims of equity;
- ❖   Consider how the two systems, equity and common law, operate in modern
  times. Note the **Judicature Act 1873**.

ANSWER

The word 'equity' in a legal context primarily means fairness or natural justice. The law
of equity developed as a fresh set of rules because of the unfair results and the limited
range of remedies available in the common-law courts.

This second set of courts known as the equity court or the Court of Chancery was under
the authority of the Lord Chancellor. The Chancellor was the King's secretary and he
ran the administrative apparatus of the state. Chancery was the office from which the
common-law writs were issued. The Lord Chancellor, who would later be the 'judge' in
the court of equity, had to decide cases relying on his conscience as a Christian.

For over five hundred years, the Court of Chancery formulated and administered the
law of equity in order to supplement the rules and procedures of the common law. At

the time, the common-law courts focused on the efficient administration of justice. As the common-law courts developed they became increasingly rigid in the way they administered justice. If a cause of action didn't fit specifically into one of the approved writs, then there was no remedy for the wrong. This emphasis on administrative efficiency on many occasions led to injustice. For example, if a person believed that the decision of the common-law court was unfair or that no appropriate remedy could be granted in a particular situation, the person could seek justice in the Court of Chancery, where, rather than emphasise legal procedures, the Court of Chancery inquired into the merits of the case.

The Chancellor also developed new equitable remedies shaped to fit each situation. Equitable orders and remedies took precedence over the legal decision and remedies of the common-law courts. Over time, several principles of equity known as 'maxims of equity' developed, a few examples of which are:

❖ Equity acts on the conscience.
❖ Equity will not suffer a wrong to be without a remedy.
❖ Equity looks to the intent rather than the form.
❖ Equitable remedies are discretionary.
❖ He who comes to equity must come with clean hands.

This resulted in great improvements to the justice system, which functioned more fairly to the benefit of society. The most powerful device available to the Court of Chancery was the injunction – to forbid someone from doing something, or command someone to do something or refrain from doing something. This power exceeded that of the common-law courts, which were only set up to award damages for wrongs already perpetrated.

However, there were still two sets of courts. The courts of equity eventually became frustrated by what they saw as the unjust decisions emanating from the common-law courts. In the sixteenth and seventeenth centuries, the equity courts began to intervene in common-law court decision-making. But as the equity courts developed, they were also not without fault, the difficulty being that 'conscience' had no limit and proceedings before the Court of Chancery dragged on and on, with cases not being decided for years and years (an expensive problem that the famous British author Charles Dickens parodied in the fictional legal case of *Jarndyce v Jarndyce* in his novel *Bleak House*).

However, eventually, in the nineteenth century the conflict between equity and common-law courts was resolved when Parliament passed the **Judicature Act 1873**. This legislation had the effect of amalgamating the Court of Chancery with the common-law courts. Common law and equity were fused into one body of law. Where there is any conflict between common-law rules and equity, equity is to prevail. Now, the rules of equity are administered in all divisions of the English courts.

Common Pitfalls ✗

Students often fudge their knowledge of the law of equity by confusing it with the concept of equality and equal rights. Make sure you know the correct subject before you begin your answer.

Aim Higher ★

Even in an essay question, whenever you can you should use case law and legislation as authority for statements of law.

QUESTION 3

Explain the English system of judicial precedent, its advantages and disadvantages, and discuss whether any alternative systems exist.

Answer Plan

This question expects a student to demonstrate a detailed knowledge of judicial precedent and the ability to analyse the pros and cons of such a system.

❖ Explain and define the terms 'judicial precedent';
❖ Explain the difference between authoritative precedents and persuasive precedents;
❖ Set out the five main levels of court for the purpose of judicial precedent;
❖ Discuss advantages such as consistency, no regional variations, flexibility, high-quality decisions and the ability to update the law;
❖ Discuss disadvantages such as the incredible volume of precedents and the need for specialist legal training to access the material;
❖ Consider alternative systems such as the civil law system and the mixed law Scottish legal system.

ANSWER

In the English legal system, a precedent is a judgment or decision of a court of law cited as an authority for deciding a similar set of facts. In other words, it is a case that serves as an authority for the legal principle embodied in the decision. The common law has developed by broadening out from precedent to precedent.

Note, however, that a particular case is only an authority for what it actually decides. 'The only use of authorities or decided cases is the establishment of some principle which the judge can follow in deciding the case before him.' (per Sir George Jessel M.R.: *Re Hallett* (1880)).

An original precedent is one that creates and applies a new rule. An authoritative precedent is one that is binding and must be followed. A persuasive precedent is one that need not be followed, but which is worth consideration.

Decisions of the House of Lords, the Supreme Court or the Court of Appeal are authoritative precedents. The High Court, however, will usually follow its own decisions (unless they are distinguishable). Commonwealth or American judgments, etc. are persuasive precedents.

Judges in lower ranking courts must follow legal principles previously formulated in higher ranking courts. This is known as the doctrine of *stare decisis*.

In summary, there are five main levels of courts for the purpose of judicial precedent. The Supreme Court is the highest ranking court in the UK, a position formerly held by the House of Lords. Its precedents bind all lower courts, but not future sittings of the Supreme Court. The Court of Appeal ranks below the Supreme Court and its decisions are binding on all inferior courts and, almost always, upon future sittings of the Court of Appeal. Decisions of Divisional Courts of the High Court are binding on future sittings of the High Court and on inferior courts. Decisions of ordinary courts of the High Court are binding on inferior courts, but not on other High Court judges. Decisions of inferior courts are not binding.

The *ratio decidendi* of a case could be defined as any statement of law that the judge applied to the facts of the case and upon which the decision in the case is based. *Obiter dicta* would include other statements of law made by the judge. Only the *ratio decidendi* of the case can be a binding precedent. *Obiter dicta* can be of persuasive authority only.

When a precedent is overruled it is changed by a higher ranking court or by a statute. A case is reversed when an appeal is successful so that the party who won in the lower court loses the appeal. An apparently binding precedent can be distinguished by a judge who refuses to follow it on the grounds that the facts of the case he is considering are materially different from the facts of the case he is distinguishing.

Some of the advantages of the system of judicial precedent include the following:

❖ The main benefit is consistency at a national level with no regional variations in the law, so that all citizens have equal rights under the law.
❖ The device of 'distinguishing' a case means that the system of precedent is not entirely inflexible. A judge lower down the hierarchy can decline to follow a precedent if s/he distinguishes its facts. A judge will say that the facts of the case s/he is considering are materially different from the facts of the case by which s/he appears to be bound. This device allows judges to avoid precedents that they consider unsuitable for the case in front of them.
❖ High-quality decisions from the more high-ranking courts are applied to all courts. Experienced appellate court judges generally make good decisions, often on complicated matters. These decisions can then be applied by much less experienced lower court judges, who do not have to give them the same consideration as to whether the principles of law involved are right or wrong. The process for the appointment of the Law Lords is very competitive and rigorous, so only the most able legal minds are selected.
❖ Unlike lower court judges, the Law Lords do not decide a case on the day. They hear the facts and the arguments in the case and then reserve their judgment. They informally discuss the matter to determine whether there is a consensus of opinion. If so, one of the judges is selected to write the judgment. If there is no consensus, the minority will write their own dissenting judgments.
❖ The system of precedent is consistent and certain, which helps lawyers to predict the outcome of most cases as most legal issues will have been previously considered by the courts and a precedent made. This certainly enables the cases to be settled without the need to go to court.
❖ Finally, the system of precedent allows for updating the law so as to adapt to business trends, resulting in the English legal system being an attractive forum for the resolution of international commercial disputes.

However, there are also several disadvantages that relate to the system of judicial precedent and these may include:

❖ Every word of every judgment made by an authoritative court might contain a precedent that would be binding on future judges. There is too much precedent material for anyone to be fully aware of it all. Indeed, many High Court judgments are not even reported in the law reports.

❖ Law reporting is carried out by private firms and is not a government responsibility. The law reporters disregard all the judgments they consider to be unimportant and not necessary to report. English case law documentation is vast. There are so many precedents that a lawyer needs specialist legal research training in order to find what s/he is looking for. Law reports are now available on the Internet, increasing the degree of accessibility.

Finally, the huge number of precedents effectively reduces the level of certainty that the system is aiming to achieve and poor decisions can remain in the law reports for a long time.

As most other countries do not use a system of judicial precedent, there are several alternatives to the system. For example, France has a codified legal system known as a civil law system. This means that the whole of the law on a particular subject such as the law of property can be found in one code. French judges, who are not barristers, but rather civil servants, are not required to interpret the codes according to precedents until those decisions have for some time unanimously interpreted the codes in the same way. Scotland has a mixed legal system. It is based on the civil law system, but has strong common-law influences. In Scotland, the system of precedent is used, but a precedent does not have the same force as in England.

Common Pitfalls ✗

Most topics and issues have advantages and disadvantages. Begin your essay by introducing your topic and explaining that you are exploring the advantages and disadvantages of this topic. When you write an essay about advantages and disadvantages, remember that you are not persuading the reader but simply giving information.

Aim Higher ★

Writing an essay about the advantages and disadvantages of an issue requires an organised outline and lists. Use transitions when writing your essay. Do not start every sentence with the words, 'one advantage' or 'one disadvantage'. Use words like despite, nevertheless, yet, however and although.

QUESTION 4

Explain the difference between the pairs of legal terminology set out below:

(a) common law and equity;
(b) criminal law and civil law;
(c) private law and public law;
(d) evidence beyond a reasonable doubt and evidence on the balance of probabilities.

Answer plan

This is a subdivided question. Answer (a) to (d) in turn, clearly identifying each section by letter and in alphabetical order. Unless you are told otherwise, it is reasonable for you to assume that each section carries equal marks. This means that each section is worth 25 per cent and you should allocate equal time to each subsection.

ANSWER

(a) 'Common law and equity' – Common law means that part of English law formulated, developed and administered by the common-law courts, originally based on the common customs of the country. The common law is 'the common sense of the community, crystallised and formulated by our forefathers'. It is not the result of legislation. The common law was limited by a system of writs. In contrast, 'equity' refers to the body of rules originally administered by the Court of Chancery. The word 'equity' in a legal context primarily means fairness or natural justice. The law of equity developed as a fresh set of rules because of the unfair results and the limited range of remedies available in the common-law courts.

(b) 'Common law and civil law' – In this context, we are concerned with the classification of law as being derived from either the common law or the civil law tradition. The common law refers to the English common law system of judicial precedent. A precedent is a court judgment or decision of a court of law, cited as an authority for deciding a similar set of facts. In other words, it is a case that serves as an authority for the legal principle embodied in the decision. The English common law system was adopted by its colonies around the world, including Canada, Australia and New Zealand among others. On the other hand, civil law refers to the Roman law legal tradition, based on the codification of legal principles. Most European countries and their former colonies around the world, for example South Africa, Brazil and others, have adopted the civil law tradition.

(c) 'Private and public law' – Private law is primarily concerned with the rights and duties of individuals towards each other. The state's involvement with private law matters between its citizens is limited to providing a civilised framework for resolving the dispute, for example a court system or tribunal system. The private citizen as opposed to the state initiates a claim or complaint. Public law, however, is concerned with the relationship between the state and its citizens. This comprises several specialist areas such as: constitutional law concerning the effects of the British Constitution; administrative law, which has developed to deal with the complaints of individuals against the decisions of the administering agency; and criminal law, whereby the state takes responsibility for the detection, prosecution and punishment of offenders.

(d) 'Evidence beyond a reasonable doubt and evidence on the balance of probabilities' – A fact is said to be proved when the court is satisfied as to its truth, and the evidence by which that result is produced is called the proof. In criminal cases, the standard of proof was formerly that the jury must find the case proved 'beyond a reasonable doubt'. It is now more usually the case that the jury is told that it must be sure of the defendant's guilt. In civil cases, while the burden of proof of a fact generally remains on the person asserting that fact, the court makes its decision on 'the balance of probabilities', that is, the evidence weighs more in favour of the claimant than of the defendant.

Common Pitfalls ✗

This short answer question requires you to provide four short answers to each of the items listed as (a) to (d). It would be a mistake not to mirror this (a) to (d) structure in writing your answer. This question comprises four parts, each involving issues of similar complexity, so make sure your answer is appropriately balanced between these parts.

Aim Higher ★

With short answer questions, examiners are generally testing your knowledge and comprehension of the topics. When you answer a question try to decide which skills are being tested.

QUESTION 5

Henry, a turkey farmer, supplied organic free-range turkeys to the Rutland Water Restaurant. Henry's turkeys have become infected with disease. The restaurant uses some infected meat for a turkey dinner for a theme night based on the American Thanksgiving celebration. Many of the guests are taken ill after the dinner, especially Jolene, a four-year-old child who becomes critically ill, is hospitalised and subsequently dies. There is no suggestion that the hospital or its staff contributed to Jolene's death.

(1) Identify the types of legal proceedings which might arise from these facts; and
(2) For each type of legal action identified in (1) above, discuss the nature of the legal liability and defences as well as the reason(s) for taking legal action.

Answer Plan

This is a typical problem question based on a set of facts that the student is required to critically analyse, while answering both (1) and (2). The best way to deal with this question is to put yourself in the position of the judge. Judges try to identify the legal issues and relevant facts and evaluate with which party liability should ultimately lie. The facts of the case are important and should be specifically dealt with in your answer.

❖ Consider the types of legal proceeding that could be initiated against (1) Henry, the supplier of the infected turkeys; (2) the Rutland Water Restaurant, which sold the meat to Jolene's parents; and (3) the Food Standards Agency, which is responsible for public health under the **Food Safety Act**;

❖ Discuss each type of legal proceeding comprehensively to include the nature of any legal liability arising, any defences and the objective of any particular party in bringing an action.

ANSWER

This case concerns food safety law and public health as well as breach of contract and the tort of negligence. We will first consider the types of legal proceedings that could be brought against Henry, the turkey farmer, followed by proceedings against the Rutland Water Restaurant and against the Food Standards Agency.

POSSIBLE PROCEEDINGS AGAINST HENRY, THE FARMER

Henry has put infected turkeys into the food chain by selling them to the Rutland Water Restaurant. Certain types of wrongdoings such as this pose a serious threat to the good order of society and are considered crimes against the whole community.

This is a public law matter arising between the state and its citizens. It being a public health issue, the state could prosecute Henry for breaches of the **Food Safety Act 1990**, in particular, selling infected meat in contravention of the food safety requirements. The burden of proof in this case would lie with the state prosecutor. She will have to prove beyond a reasonable doubt that Henry had supplied infected meat. If this is established, Henry will be convicted and sentenced. He could face being ordered to pay a fine (a civil penalty), or even be imprisoned as the supply of meat resulted in the death of Jolene, a young girl (criminal penalty).

In addition, the Rutland Water Restaurant could sue Henry for damages (financial compensation) in the civil courts for breach of contract, due to his failure to supply meat of good quality and for the costs that the Restaurant has incurred as a result of the breach.

If the Restaurant is sued in the civil courts for product liability and negligence causing personal injury to Jolene, it may join Henry as a party to the action, as he also contributed to the cause of Jolene's death.

POSSIBLE ACTIONS AGAINST THE RUTLAND WATER RESTAURANT

As a food retailer, the Restaurant is required to sell safe food to its customers. Following an investigation by food health scientists, the Restaurant could be sued by the State under the **Food Safety Act 1990** as a matter of public law. However, the Restaurant may be able to rely on the due diligence defence under the Act. This defence provides that if all reasonable precautions had been taken and all due diligence exercised to avoid the commission of the offence, then the defendant will not be liable.

Jolene's family will have to sue the Restaurant in the civil courts as this is a dispute between private individuals, namely the family versus the owners of the Restaurant. The purpose of the action is to remedy the wrong suffered. Although a civil action for financial compensation (damages) will never bring Jolene back to life, this is the best way for the law to remedy the injured party. The family might seek compensation for medical bills, lost wages during their daughter's illness and Jolene's wrongful death. Family members would also sue for funeral expenses and all other expenses directly.

The family will have to prove that the turkey Jolene ate was the cause of her death. This will require scientific and medical lead evidence to be presented at trial, which proves that on the balance of probabilities the infected turkey meat was the cause of death. It may be that other people were adversely affected by consuming the infected turkey meat and this would be good evidence to present to support the claim of negligence.

POSSIBLE ACTION AGAINST THE FOOD STANDARDS AGENCY

The State, via the Food Standards Agency, could also be sued by Jolene's family and/or the Restaurant for failing to investigate or detect the infection at Henry's farm. If prima facie evidence is available, then this would be a public administrative law matter involving a formal complaint against a decision of a state agency. The standard of proof would be the civil standard.

Common Pitfalls ✗

The most common error made by students is to cite the relevant case law and legislation but not use the law to advise on an outcome. In other words, read the facts carefully and then apply the law to those facts.

Aim Higher ★

The final sentence of the question tells you what to do. Provide an objective view of the law and don't favour the victims just because they have suffered.

QUESTION 6

In what circumstances is a court bound by previous decisions and why is this doctrine of *stare decisis* effective?

Answer Plan

- ❖ Examine the doctrine of *stare decisis* in the context of the court hierarchy with the Supreme Court at the apex.
- ❖ Explain the meaning of *obiter dictum*.
- ❖ Consider the effectiveness of the doctrine of *stare decisis*.

ANSWER

To determine in what circumstances a court is bound by a previous decision, we have to examine the doctrine of binding precedence or *stare decisis*. The doctrine of *stare* decisis is the sacred principle of English law by which precedents are authoritative, binding and must be followed. Within the hierarchy of the English courts, a decision by a higher court will be binding on those courts lower than it and usually a court of equal standing. Adherence to precedent is called *stare decisis* ('to stand by the decision').

The highest court in England is the Supreme Court – it binds all the other courts and it is the only court that could depart from its previous judgments. However, the Supreme Court is now bound by European law by virtue of the UK's membership of the European Union. Until 1966, the House of Lords (the UK's highest court prior to the establishment of the Supreme Court in 2009) was bound by its previous decisions, except where such decisions were made *per curiam*. In 1996, the House of Lords, by way of a formal practice statement, declared that it was no longer bound by its own previous decisions. For example, their Lordships overturned the decision in the criminal case of *R v R* (1991) and declared that rape within marriage is now a crime. Their Lordships realised that adherence to precedence in every instance may lead to injustice. However, their Lordships also declared that this is not to interfere with the use of precedence in the lower courts. This explains the reason why the Court of Appeal, the Divisional High Court, the High Court and the subordinate courts such as the Crown and magistrates' courts cannot overturn decisions that they had previously and incorrectly made.

The *ratio decidendi* is the legal principle applied and the reason for the judgment. The *ratio decidendi* is the most important part of the judgment and a judge would consider it if s/he wants to adopt an earlier judgment and be bound by it.

Obiter dictum, however, is just something said 'by the way'. It is an observation by a judge on a legal question suggested by a case before him/her, but not arising in such a manner as to require a decision. It is therefore not binding as a precedent. But there is no justification for regarding as *obiter dictum* a reason given by a judge for his/her decision because s/he has given another reason also.

The doctrine of *stare decisis* is effective, first, because it promotes uniformity of law within a jurisdiction, makes the court system more efficient and makes the law more predictable for individuals and businesses. The doctrine brings a great deal of certainty to the English legal system as litigants will be confident that cases with similar facts might be decided in the same way. A court may later change or reverse its legal reasoning if a new case is presented to it and change is warranted. This is because the judge has the ability to distinguish a case if s/he does not want to be bound by precedents and make the doctrine not entirely rigid. Second, the doctrine is efficient because it assists subordinate courts with less qualified legal personnel to adopt precedents that have been made by very qualified judges; therefore, the subordinate court judges are not required to constantly try to formulate and interpret the law.

Finally, without the doctrine of *stare decisis* there would be no stability in our system of jurisprudence. *Stare decisis* channels the law.

Common Pitfalls ✗

Make sure you carefully explain, in plain English, the legal terminology in Latin to show the examiner that you clearly understand the terms.

Aim Higher ★

From your reading and study, think of and discuss the circumstances in which a court is bound by its earlier decisions and which courts are not bound.

The Courts, Small Business and the Law-Making Process

INTRODUCTION

A court is a place where justice is administered. A small business is most likely to make or defend a claim in the county court. A county court deals exclusively with civil law cases, for example breaches of contract, wrongs (called torts) and property matters. The county court is presided over by a judge (referred to as a circuit judge) without a jury. The main business applications are claims with a financial value of not more than £5,000 (or a larger sum if the parties consent to the case being allocated to what is known as the small claims track). The county court now has an online service, which can be accessed for making monetary claims, at: https://www.moneyclaim.gov.uk.

Other jurisdictions specifically relevant to business include equity matters such as for breach of trust by trustees or breach of contract for undue influence, bankruptcies, company winding-up and consumer credit. These disputes will normally be heard in the High Court (Chancery Division).

The Court of Appeal is the next rung up the court hierarchy ladder. Its decisions are binding on all lower courts and on future sittings of the Court of Appeal itself. In terms of precedent, the Court of Appeal is the most important court as it hears several thousand cases per year.

The Supreme Court is the highest court in Great Britain and Northern Ireland. It replaced the House of Lords on 1 October 2009, when the 11 Law Lords who used to sit in the House of Lords became the first Supreme Court justices. There are now 12 Supreme Court justices who hear about 100 cases per year.

The **Civil Procedure Rules (CPR) 1998** attempt to reduce the amount of delay and complexity that can exist in the civil justice system. The Rules give the judge in the court in which the proceedings begin the power to determine a suitable venue for the case before the case is heard. The judge can allocate the case to the small claims track (for claims not exceeding £5,000), the fast track (for claims over £5,000 but not exceeding £15,000), or the multitrack (for claims over £15,000). Where the claim is over £50,000 it will be held in the High Court.

The courts are involved with interpreting and applying the law as set out in legislation. Legislation is law enacted by the Queen in Parliament in the form of Acts of Parliament or statutes. Parliament is made up of two chambers: the House of Commons and the House of Lords. There are several stages for a legislative proposal to be translated into an Act of Parliament. The proposal for a new law is known as a Bill. In practice most Bills start their journey in the House of Commons and then proceed to the House of Lords before receiving Royal Assent. The detailed procedure is set out below.

HOUSE OF COMMONS

❖ First reading (title of Bill read out, printed and published);
❖ Second reading (purpose of the Bill is explained and general principles are debated);
❖ Committee stage (the Bill is examined clause by clause and any amendments are voted on);
❖ Report stage (the Bill is formally reported to the House of Commons);
❖ Third reading (the Bill is debated again and only minor amendments can be made).

HOUSE OF LORDS

The Bill goes through a procedure similar to the House of Commons procedure.

ROYAL ASSENT

A formality as the Queen's approval is never refused.

The Bill is now an Act of Parliament. The sovereign law-making powers of the Queen in Parliament mean that the courts cannot question the validity of a statute (i.e. the way it was made).

QUESTION 7

The process of bringing, maintaining and defending a legal case in court is called litigation. For business people, litigation is a difficult, time-consuming and costly process that must comply with procedural rules. This usually requires professional legal advice. Discuss the steps involved in the trial of a legal matter in a civil court.

Answer Plan

This essay question requires the student to demonstrate knowledge of the trial process and the key stages in a trial from start to finish.

❖ Set out an explanation of the purpose of a civil legal action (examples might include contract, tort and property law matters), the parties, the case title and where a civil action will be heard at first instance.
❖ Discuss the burden of proof and the civil standard.
❖ Explain the modern system of case management and the fast-track, small-claims-track and multi-track procedures.
❖ Discuss the workings of the opening statement, the presentation of the claimant's case, the presentation of the defendant's case, cross-examination, closing arguments, entry of judgment and sanctions (e.g. damages, injunction, specific performance, rescission).

ANSWER

Many of the laws affecting business people are part of the civil law, especially contract, tort and property law. In civil proceedings, private disputes between individuals are heard by a judge, who also decides the legal outcome of the matter. In legal terminology, a claimant sues a defendant in the civil courts and the case title will be, for example, *Smith v Jones*. The civil courts – that is, the county court or the High Court – are where the action is heard. The High Court and the county courts are a single jurisdiction operating to a common set of procedural rules known as the **Civil Procedures Rules (CPR) 1998**.

When a case is brought, it will be allocated to the most appropriate court. Cases are allocated to one of three tracks, depending on their value and complexity.

The fast track is for claims between £5,000 and £15,000. The cases are heard by the county court within 30 weeks. The usual hearing time is three hours, with an absolute maximum of one day.

The small claims track is for all claims up to £5,000 except for personal injury and housing cases where the limit is £1,000.

The multi-track is for all claims over £15,000 and for complex cases of less than £15,000. The High Court deals with multi-track cases.

In terms of the actual legal proceedings for the trial of the case, each party's barrister is allowed to make an opening statement. The barrister usually summarises the main factual and legal issues of the case and describes why s/he believes the client's position is valid. The information given in the opening statement is not considered as evidence.

The claimant bears the burden of proof to persuade the judge (the trier of fact) of the merits of her/his case. This is called the claimant's case. The claimant's barrister calls witnesses to give evidence on oath. After the witness has been sworn in, the claimant's barrister examines (i.e. questions) the witness and this is called 'direct examination'. Documents and other evidence can be introduced through each witness. After the claimant's barrister has completed her/his questions, the defendant's barrister can question the witness. This is called 'cross-examination'. The defendant's barrister can ask questions only about the subjects that were brought up during the direct examination. After the defendant's barrister completes his/her questions, the claimant's barrister can again question the witness and this is called 're-examination'.

The defendant's case begins after the claimant has concluded his/her case. The defendant's case must: (1) rebut the claimant's evidence; (2) prove any affirmative defences asserted by the defendant; and (3) prove any allegations contained in the defendant's counterclaim against the claimant. The defendant's witnesses are examined in the same way as the claimant's witnesses.

At the conclusion of the presentation of the evidence, each party's barrister is allowed to make a closing argument. Both barristers try to convince the judge to render a verdict for their clients by pointing out the strengths in the client's case and the weaknesses in the other side's case. Information given by the barristers in their closing arguments is not evidence.

The claimant will be successful if s/he can prove her/his case on the balance of probabilities. This means that the evidence weighs more in favour of the claimant than of the defendant. If the claimant wins their action, the defendant is said to be liable and the court will order an appropriate remedy, such as damages (financial compensation) or an injunction (an order to do or not to do something). If the claimant is not successful, the defendant is found not liable and the claimant may have to pay all or a proportion of the defendant's legal costs.

Common Pitfalls ✗

The temptation here is to begin to discuss actual cases that the student has studied or read about in the news, rather than the procedure for bringing a case to court. The question is examining the student's understanding of the procedure within the legal system.

Aim Higher ★

Put on your commercial hat and think about what remedies the claimant will want the court to grant, e.g. damages, injunctions, etc.

QUESTION 8

(a) Oakham Medical Centre Ltd has a claim for £40,000 against Edmondthorpe Medical Supplies Ltd for the delivery of defective heart-rate monitors. There are some difficult questions of fact to be decided in the claim, involving scientific and medical evidence. Advise Oakham Medical Centre whether the claim will be heard in the county court or the High Court and why.

(b) Oakham Medical Centre Ltd has a claim against a private patient, Miss Clarke, for £3,000 for physiotherapy treatment services. Advise Oakham Medical Centre whether the claim will be heard in the county court or the High Court and why.

Answer Plan

This is a subdivided question. Answer (a) and (b) in turn, clearly identifying each section by letter and in alphabetical order. Unless you are told otherwise, it is reasonable for you to assume that each section carries equal marks. This means that each section is worth 50 per cent and you should allocate equal time to each subsection.

(a) Identify the legal cause of action, e.g. breach of contract and the appropriate court to bringing legal action.

(b) Consider the value of the claim and the appropriate court to commence legal proceedings.

ANSWER

(a) In this case, where there is a claim for breach of contract amounting to £40,000, the claimant, Oakham Medical Centre Ltd, has the choice of beginning the claim in the High Court or the county court. In such a case, under procedural rules, the claim may be started in the High Court if there are complex facts and legal issues to be determined and/or the claim is important to the public in general. Here, we are told that there are some difficult questions of fact to be decided in the claim involving scientific and medical evidence concerning a highly technical heart-rate monitor. This will require expert reports and testimony from expert witnesses. It is likely that the hearing will take longer than the maximum one day allocated to a case in the county court. Accordingly, it is appropriate for the claimant's solicitor to commence the case in the High Court.

(b) If all attempts to get payment fail, a business may have to consider a claim through the legal process. Essentially, Oakham Medical Centre Ltd – the claimant – will need to make a claim against Miss Clarke to recover the debt that she has so far refused to pay. Given that, so far as is known, the defendant, Miss Clarke, has adequate resources to meet the claim, one option is the small claims procedure. There is no small claims court as such. However, all small claims are dealt with in county courts. A claim such as this with a financial value of not more than £5,000 will be allocated to the small claims track. Most business litigants will choose to instruct a solicitor to act for them, but note that there is a 'no-costs' rule for small claims, so that the successful litigant will not usually recover any legal costs. This is part of an intentional policy to reassure litigants that they will not be at risk of paying substantial legal costs if they lose their case. A district judge usually hears small claims with appeal to a circuit judge. Sometimes in a small claim the defendant may make a counterclaim against the claimant. In deciding whether the case is to be heard on the small claims track, the value of any counterclaim must also be taken into account.

Common Pitfalls ✗

Always make a plan before you answer a problem question. Read the question a couple of times, underlining important words and phrases. Confirm what the question wants you to do. As this is quite a short problem question, the examiner will expect an accurate, succinctly written answer.

QUESTION 9

X Ltd is suing Y Ltd, claiming contract damages for £5,009. Y Ltd has decided to contest
the matter and defend the claim in court. The claim is not in respect of personal
injuries. Advise X Ltd as to in which courts the claim might be tried. To which courts
might an appeal be made, if all possible appeals were made?

Answer Plan

This is a practical problem question designed so that the student can demonstrate
his or her knowledge of case management and the three tracks to which the court
may allocate a claim.

❖   Classify the claim as civil or criminal.
❖   Consider the county court and the High Court's jurisdiction.
❖   Consider the appropriate track for the claim to be allocated to a court.
❖   Analyse whether it would be advisable for X Ltd to reduce its claim so that
     the matter could be allocated to the small claims track.

ANSWER

This is a business dispute involving a claim for breach of contract. It is therefore a civil
matter and civil procedure applies. If a civil dispute cannot be settled between the
parties and reaches the stage of litigation, it will commence either in the county court
or in the High Court. The county court has unlimited jurisdiction to hear a contract
case. The High Court also has unlimited jurisdiction to hear contract cases as long as
the case involves a claim for a sufficiently large sum of money. However, if the claim
includes a claim for personal injuries (and X's claim does not), the claim must be at
least £50,000. The value of the action is the amount that the claimant reasonably
expects to recover. In cases in which there is no claim for personal injuries, two
general rules apply in the allocation of cases between the county court and the High
Court. First, cases in which the claim is for less than £25,000 should be heard in the
county court. Second, cases in which the claim is for over £50,000 should be heard in
the High Court.

Note that if a litigant, such as X Ltd, fails to follow the correct procedure, it is possible that its claim will be struck out. However, X Ltd does have another option to recover damages for breach of the contract as detailed below.

In this instance, if the claim is for only £5,009, the case should be tried in the county court at first instance. The circuit judge hears more complex claims and those in which the amount claimed is greater. If the amount in dispute is between £5,000 and £15,000 the case might be heard by either a district judge or a circuit judge. Straightforward claims for not more than £5,000 are generally allocated to the small claims track. It might be more practical for X Ltd to consider reducing its claim to £5,000 in order for the matter to be allocated to the small claims track. The advantage of the small claims track is that the case will only involve one hearing before a district judge. No expert evidence will be admitted in a small claim hearing unless the court consents, and such consent will not usually be granted. The hearing is informal and the strict rules of evidence do not apply. The judge will probably appoint each side the same amount of time to present their evidence and give an immediate decision at the conclusion of the case. Each side will pay its own costs. The only costs recoverable will usually be the costs involved in issuing the claim.

An appeal against the decision of the county court circuit judge can be made to a High Court judge. An appeal against a decision of the High Court can be made to the Court of Appeal and from there to the Supreme Court if necessary.

Common Pitfalls ✘

Ensure you show that you understand the relevant aspects of the English legal system in your answer, namely the hierarchy of the courts as well as the importance of procedure within the court system.

Aim Higher ★

Think commercially about the options available to X Ltd. It may be wise to advise X Ltd that it is preferable to reduce its claim so that the matter could be allocated to the small claims track in order to be dealt with in a more timely and cost effective way.

QUESTION 10

Describe the relationship between the judiciary and Parliament in respect of Acts of Parliament.

Answer Plan

In this essay question students should:

❖ introduce the concept of law-making in the English legal system by contrasting it with the European civil law-making system;

❖ define and explain the meaning of each of the terms: 'judiciary', 'Parliament' and 'Acts of Parliament';

❖ evaluate the law-making role of judges contrasted with that of Parliament;

❖ analyse Parliament's role in law-making – legislation is the name given to law made by Parliament;

❖ explain Acts of Parliament and how a law is made;

❖ explain the rules of statutory interpretation used by judges and *Pepper v Hart* (1993).

ANSWER

The role of law-making is an important feature of every country's legal system. In most European countries, the law has been codified and the whole of the law on a particular subject, for example, contract law, can be found in one document. In European countries, judges interpret the legal code and do not deliberately set out to create new laws. However, in England and Wales the bulk of the law has been made by judges in individual cases. The decisions of judges in the High Court, the Court of Appeal and the Supreme Court must be followed by lower-ranking judges, so these senior judges are constantly creating the law.

A judge is an officer of the Crown who sits to administer justice according to law. However, the courts frequently have to interpret, that is, decide the meaning of statutes, particularly where they are not using clear and well-established rules of statutory interpretation to resolve ambiguity as to the meaning of words or phrases in a statute. Let us now explore precisely how Parliament makes law before turning to the way in which judges interpret statutes to create law.

A statute is the ultimate source of law. The theory of Parliamentary sovereignty holds that the UK Parliament can pass any law it wishes to pass and that no Parliament can bind later Parliaments in such a way as to limit their power to legislate. Parliament is the sovereign legislative authority on the constitution, consisting of the Queen, the House of Lords and the House of Commons. A Bill that successfully passes through the House of Commons and the House of Lords and has received the Royal Assent becomes an Act of Parliament. The sovereign law-making powers of the Queen in Parliament mean that the validity of a statement (i.e. the way it was made) cannot be questioned by a judge in court. Nevertheless, the courts can exercise considerable influence over how the enacted law is interpreted and applied to practical problems. Eventually, every Act of Parliament will be analysed by the judges in the course of cases that appear before them. It is the task of the judge to decide the meaning of and to construe the words used by Parliament in order to ascertain what Parliament intended. There are two types of rules of interpretation: statutory or common law rules.

STATUTORY RULES OF INTERPRETATION

Modern Acts usually contain an interpretation section that defines certain key words under that Act. In addition, the **Interpretation Act 1978** sets out certain basic rules of interpretation for all Acts. For example, **s 6** provides that words in the singular shall include the plural and words in the plural shall include the singular, unless the contrary intention is indicated. Finally, the Act in question itself may be useful as an intrinsic aid. The courts may consider the long title of the Act and its preamble.

COMMON LAW RULES OF INTERPRETATION

Over time, judges have developed their own rules and methods of interpreting a statute. Several approaches are acceptable and the judge is free to choose the approach he or she feels is most appropriate to the case before him/her. These common law rules of interpretation are:

1. Literal rule – where possible the words of a statute must be interpreted literally, save where this would produce unintended consequences or absurdity.
2. Golden rule – where the words of a statute are capable of two or more meanings, the judge must adopt the interpretation which produces the least absurd result.
3. Mischief rule – the court must consider the Act to see what 'mischief' or 'defect' in the common law the Act was passed to remedy and then interpret the words of the Act in the light of that knowledge.
4. *Ejusdem generis* rule – where general words follow particular words, the court should interpret the general words as meaning persons or things of the same class or genus; for example, if the Act states 'cats and dogs or other animals', the general words 'other animals' should be construed as meaning all kinds of domesticated animals and not wild animals.

In addition, there are several presumptions that a court must adhere to when determining the meaning of words in a statute. A court assumes that an Act:

❖ is not retrospective, that is, it does not backdate the change in the law;
❖ does not bind the Crown;
❖ does not alter the common law;
❖ does not restrict personal liberty;
❖ does not create criminal liability unless *mens rea* is present.

Finally, judges may also use certain extrinsic sources of information about an Act, for example, international treaties and conventions and Law Commission Reports. As a result of the decision in the case of *Pepper v Hart* (1993), the House of Lords held that a court could refer to Hansard where:

(i)   the legislation is ambiguous or obscure or where a literal interpretation would lead to an absurdity;
(ii) the material referred to consists of statements by a minister or other promoter of the Bill, together with such other parliamentary material as is necessary to understand the statements and their effects;
(iii) the statements relied on are clear.

However, it should be borne in mind by the courts and the judges interpreting legislation that the intention of Parliament is expressed in the language used in its enactments. The role of judges is a unique feature in the common law legal system.

Common Pitfalls ✘

Be careful not to focus solely on the role of judges in the law-making process; it is equally important to discuss legislation: Acts of Parliament. Once these two concepts have been explained, the student should turn to an analysis of the role of the judiciary in interpreting legislation.

Aim Higher ★

Add value to your answer by setting out the rules used by judges to assist with statutory interpretation as well as any relevant case law such as *Pepper v Hart*.

QUESTION 11

Explain the differences between the following pairs of legal terminology:

(a) a Bill and a statute;

(b) the House of Commons and the House of Lords;

(c) the golden rule and the mischief rule;

(d) the County Court and the Supreme Court.

Answer Plan

This is a subdivided question. Answer (a) to (d) in turn, clearly identifying each section by letter and in alphabetical order. Unless you are told otherwise, it is reasonable for you to assume that each section carries equal marks. This means that each section is worth 25 per cent and you should allocate equal time to each subsection.

ANSWER

(a) **A Bill and a statute** – To become a statute, a draft proposal of the legislation, known as a Bill, must pass through both Houses of Parliament and then gain the Royal Assent. Many Bills achieve this without significant alteration. Others have to be amended to gain parliamentary approval. Some Bills do not become statutes at all. Once the Bill has received the Royal Assent, it becomes a statute, which the courts must enforce. A statute is the ultimate source of law. The theory of the sovereignty of Parliament provides that the UK Parliament can pass any law it wishes and no Parliament can bind a later Parliament in such a way as to limit their powers to legislate. Judges may not consider the validity of statutes, but they are compelled to apply them. Statutes remain in force indefinitely or until they are repealed. A statute loses none of its authority merely because it has been dormant for many years. For example, in *R v Duncan* (1944) the defendant was convicted of fortune-telling in contravention of the **Witchcraft Act 1735**, even though the statute had not been used for many years.

(b) **The House of Commons and the House of Lords** – Parliament is made up of two chambers: the House of Commons and the House of Lords. The Commons consists of 650 elected Members of Parliament (MPs) who represent an area of the country called a constituency. Under plans agreed by Parliament in early 2011, the total number of Members of Parliament will be reduced by 8 per cent to 6,000 members by 2015. Constituencies across the UK will be redrawn to ensure they comply with new rules standardising their population size at between 72,810 and 80,473. The political party that can command a majority of votes in the Commons forms the Government and its leader becomes the Prime Minister. Ministers are appointed by the Prime Minister to take charge of the various government departments. The most important ministers form the Cabinet, which is the group of people responsible for formulating Government policy. The House of Lords, on the other hand, is not an elected body. Following changes made by the **House of Lords Act 1999**, the House of Lords is composed of life peers, hereditary peers, 26 Law Lords and spiritual peers (the Archbishops of Canterbury and York) and the 24 bishops of the Church of England. Under the **Constitutional Reform Act 2005**, the Lord Chancellor will continue to be a government minister at the Cabinet level with responsibility for the judiciary and the court system, but his judicial functions are transferred to the President of the Courts of England and Wales.

(c) **The golden rule and the mischief rule** – The golden rule and the mischief rule are methods of statutory interpretation used by judges. Most judges adopt the golden rule (the purposive approach) to statutory interpretation. The judges use the golden rule to give the words in a statute their ordinary, literal meaning, but only to the extent that this would not produce an absurd result: *R v Allen* (1872). Another rule of statutory interpretation – the mischief rule – holds that the judge can take into account the common law 'mischief' that the statute set out to remedy: *Smith v Hughes* (1960). It is difficult to predict which rule a court will adopt, although the golden rule is usually preferred over the literal rule. However, a court is free to adopt elements of both approaches to statutory interpretation.

(d) **The county court and the Supreme Court** – The county court is what is known as an 'inferior' court. Decisions of inferior courts are not binding on any other courts. A judge sitting in the county court does not make precedents. On top of the English court hierarchy sits the Supreme Court. The Supreme Court comprises twelve judges, five of whom sit in any one case. Law Lords are not bound by any previous precedents and, furthermore, their decisions are binding on all the courts beneath them. In practice, the Law Lords tend to follow their previous decisions unless there is a good reason not to. The Supreme Court replaced the House of Lords on 1 October 2009. The Supreme Court gives judges greater independence from government; nevertheless, the Supreme Court has no power to overturn a statute. The Supreme Court is housed within a new building, not within the Houses of Parliament.

Common Pitfalls ✗

This short answer question requires you to provide four short answers to each of the sections listed as (a) to (d). It would be a mistake not to mirror this (a) to (d) structure in writing your answer. This question comprises four parts, each involving issues of similar complexity, so make sure your answer is appropriately balanced between these parts.

Aim Higher ★

With short answer questions, examiners are generally testing your knowledge and comprehension of the topics. When you answer a question try to decide which skills are being tested.

The Legal Profession

INTRODUCTION

In England and Wales, there are essentially two main branches of the legal profession – solicitors and barristers.

'Solicitors' advise individuals and organisations on legal matters and ensure that their clients act in accordance with the law. Solicitors usually work in an office rather than in court. There are over 116,000 practising solicitors in England and Wales, governed by the Solicitors Regulation Authority (SRA). Almost 45 per cent of solicitors are women and over 11 per cent of all solicitors are from ethnic minority groups.

'Barristers' provide two main services – advocacy (representing clients in court) and giving specialist opinions on complex legal matters. They generally receive instructions through solicitors. There are around 12,000 barristers practising in the UK, governed by the Bar Standards Board. About 68 per cent of barristers are men and 11 per cent are from ethnic minority groups.

The distinction between solicitors and barristers has blurred slightly over time. Since the 1990s solicitors have been able to represent clients in the lower courts (such as magistrates' courts) and, if they have enough experience and gain specific 'higher rights' qualifications, they can become 'solicitor advocates' and represent clients in higher courts (such as Crown Courts or the High Court).

Barristers are not allowed to form partnerships. Groups of barristers share offices called 'chambers' and are allocated work by a barrister's clerk, who is also responsible for negotiating the barrister's fees. A barrister can only be employed by a solicitor and can only meet the client he represents if the solicitor is also present.

Queen's Counsel (QC) or a 'silk': senior barristers are known as Queen's Counsel and they generally appear with a junior barrister assisting them. The Queen's Counsel Selection Panel makes the award of Queen's Counsel. The Selection Panel is supported by its own Secretariat, which aims to serve the public interest by offering a fair and transparent means of identifying excellence in advocacy in the higher courts of England and Wales.

Many solicitors and barristers work in industry or commerce or for local government or the Civil Service. However, the **Legal Services Act 2007** has reformed the way legal services in England and Wales are regulated and puts the consumer's interest at the heart of the regulatory framework. The Act set out the framework for reform, which included setting up a Legal Services Board (LSB) and an Office for Legal Complaints (OLC) and enabling legal services to be provided under new business structures. The Act also now allows barristers and solicitors to work together in partnership.

Alternative business structures (ABS) enable consumers to obtain services from one business entity, which brings together lawyers and non-lawyers – increasing competitiveness and improving services. In the near future, the Act will also allow legal services firms to have up to 25 per cent non-lawyer partners before the full ABS regulatory structure is implemented, and will allow different kinds of lawyers to form firms together. Proper regulation is vital to ensure a robust, independent legal profession, with high ethical standards.

THE JUDICIARY

The English legal system has developed over hundreds of years and this development influences the way the judiciary perform their duties. For hundreds of years the overriding principle of the English legal system has been that judges are independent of government. That means they make their decisions without interference from the government or the executive. Judges also do not get involved with politics.

When judges are sworn in they take two oaths/affirmations. The first is the oath of allegiance and the second the judicial oath; these are collectively referred to as the judicial oath.

The **Constitutional Reform Act 2005** introduced an important change to the role of the Lord Chancellor – a politician and member of the Cabinet. On 3 April 2006, when the Act came into force, the Lord Chief Justice became head of the judiciary of England and Wales, a role previously held by the Lord Chancellor. The Lord Chief Justice is also President of the Courts of England and Wales. The current Lord Chief Justice is Lord Judge, who was appointed in October 2008.

The judiciary of England and Wales can be separated into the following types:

❖ Heads of Division
❖ Lords Justices of Appeal

❖ High Court judges
❖ Circuit judges
❖ Recorders
❖ District and deputy district judges
❖ District and deputy district judges (magistrates' courts)
❖ Justices of the peace (or 'lay magistrates')

In 2010, there were ten Lord Justices of the Supreme Court and 36 Lord Justices of Appeal in office. The High Court judges deal with the more complicated and difficult cases, for example company law, probate and tax, among others. Eighteen High Court judges were assigned to the Chancery Division, 71 to the Queen's Bench Division and 18 to the Family Division. Sir Nicholas Bratza is a Judge of the European Court of Human Rights. In terms of diversity, approximately 20 per cent of judges are female and 5 per cent are from ethnic minorities.

Finally, there are approximately 30,000 lay magistrates, who are not paid a salary. Magistrates are not legally qualified, but do receive legal training on appointment. Lay magistrates must live and work in the area where they sit to hear cases and must have a good knowledge of the local community, a good character and personal integrity and be between the ages of 27 and 65. Members of the police and armed forces are not eligible for appointment.

QUESTION 12

Critically analyse the 'cab rank rule' and explain how it operates.

Answer Plan

This essay question expects the student to demonstrate a knowledge of the 'cab rank rule' and how the rule impacts on the role of the practising barrister.

❖ Define and explain the 'cab rank rule'.
❖ Illustrate with an example.
❖ Discuss the principles underpinning this long-standing rule.
❖ Consider when a barrister can lawfully withhold his or her services.
❖ Briefly refer to reform.

ANSWER

The standard question for barristers is: how can you act for someone you know or suspect must be guilty? The 'cab rank rule' governs barristers' acceptance of instructions from clients. Like a licensed taxi, barristers in England and Wales must adhere to the rule that in theory it requires a barrister to take the next case that comes along, whatever it is and however distasteful. The rule derives its name from the tradition by which a Hackney Carriage driver at the head of a queue of taxicabs is supposed to take the first passenger requesting a ride. By way of example, this means that an ardent feminist barrister would represent a serial rapist. Many advocates pride themselves on taking cases on both sides of the fence and on not solely taking prosecution or defence briefs.

The principle underpinning the 'cab rank rule' is the idea that everyone deserves the right to be defended and so the 'cab rank rule' is one of the legal system's oldest and fairest laws. Furthermore, the English system is premised on the notion that the accused is innocent until proven guilty beyond all reasonable doubt. The burden of proof lies with the prosecution to prove its case against the accused. Accordingly, a defendant is entitled to be properly represented in court and to have his or her case put forward as well as possible.

Another rationale behind the principle is that anyone in the land can have access to the best brains at the Bar. Solicitors in remote corners of the British Isles can instruct leading counsel of their choice in London, Leeds or Nottingham.

In practice, though, barristers who are in demand can plead prior engagement and work commitments and they can select which cases they are available to take on. Furthermore, some barristers' fees are beyond the means of many clients, and barristers' clerks, who arrange what case a barrister can take, are skilled at deflecting unwanted cases.

Nevertheless, barristers must not withhold their services on the grounds that:

❖ the case is 'objectionable' to him or her or to any section of the public; or
❖ the client's beliefs are unacceptable; or
❖ the source of financing provided to the client (e.g. Legal Aid) is objectionable.

When is it lawful for a barrister to turn down a brief? There are wide grounds for refusal. A barrister must refuse work if s/he lacks experience or competence in a case. A barrister may turn down a brief is s/he feels s/he will not have time to prepare the case properly and would be professionally embarrassed or if the fee is inadequate.

In 2008, the Bar Standards Board – the barristers' regulatory body – published a consultation paper entitled *Acceptance and Return of Instructions*, initiating a debate on when barristers can decline to be instructed on a case or withdraw from it. The purpose of the consultation is to consider whether to amend the Code of Conduct for the Bar.

In conclusion, in the absence of such a rule it might be difficult for an unpopular person to obtain legal representation, and barristers who act for such people might be criticised for doing so. In 1999, Lord Irvine, the then Lord Chancellor, said: 'The "cab rank" rule is one of the glories of the Bar. It underscores that every member of the Bar is obliged, without fear or favour, to represent clients who offer themselves, regardless of how unpopular they may be in the community or elsewhere.' Notwithstanding the Lord Chancellor's view, the cab rank rule is not universally admired and in 2010 the Law Society of England and Wales said: 'The Society questions whether the cab rank rule remains a necessary and proportionate rule for the Bar at a time when there is increasing competition for advocacy services.'

Common Pitfalls ✗

Avoid stating a lot of past case laws as the question does not call for this. Rather the question invites the student to demonstrate their understanding of a particular branch of the legal profession and a rule of ethics in relation to their conduct.

Aim Higher ★

Demonstrate a good understanding of the 'cab rank rule' by explaining it in plain English and illustrating it with a practical example to confirm your understanding. Add value to your answer by providing critical analysis of the rule.

QUESTION 13

Briefly explain the role of each of the following members of the legal profession:

(a) Solicitor;
(b) Barrister;
(c) Notary public;
(d) Legal executive;
(e) Licensed conveyancer.

> **Answer Plan**
>
> This is a subdivided question requiring the student to demonstrate general knowledge and understanding. Answer (a) to (e) in turn, clearly identifying each section by letter in alphabetical order. Unless you are told otherwise, it is reasonable for you to assume that each section carries equal marks. This means that each section is worth 20 per cent and you should allocate equal time to each subsection.

ANSWER

(a) 'Solicitor' – A solicitor is akin to a general practitioner (GP) in the medical profession. Solicitors tend to practise in a partnership with other solicitors or in a sole practice. They are the first port of call for a client requiring professional legal advice. Solicitors provide an all-round legal service and their work is extremely varied, including, but not limited to, criminal law, family law, wills and estates, and business law. Commercial work carried out for business clients may involve forming companies, drafting partnership agreements, applying for licences, drafting contracts or advising on tax matters for example. In terms of litigation, solicitors gather evidence and interview witnesses. Suitably qualified solicitors may now appear in court as advocates, although it is common practice for a solicitor to brief a barrister to appear in court on behalf of the client. The Solicitors Regulation Authority is the governing body for solicitors and it controls the legal education, admission to the profession and professional standards.

(b) 'Barrister' – Barristers are specialist advocates who represent a client in court or in a tribunal to present their case. A barrister's work involves more than advocacy as they also carry out legal research and provide opinions on difficult questions of law. They also assist to draft legal documents. A Queen's Counsel (QC) is a senior barrister who has at least 15 to 20 years' experience and is appointed by an independent selection panel, which includes laypeople. Consequently, QCs are more expensive and usually specialise in particular areas of law. They normally only appear in court together with a junior barrister, to whom the QC will delegate certain aspects of the case to handle. All barristers are governed by the General Council of the Bar. Admission to the Bar is controlled by the four Inns of Court (Inner Temple, Middle Temple, Gray's Inn and Lincoln's Inn).

(c) 'Notary public' – A notary public is a qualified lawyer and an officer of the law, who is authorised to attest the signing (execution) of any deeds or writings, or to make certified copies of them in order to render them authentic, especially for use abroad. In England and Wales a notary public is appointed by the Archbishop of Canterbury and can be removed from office by the Court of Faculties. Notaries also prepare wills and probate documents, administer oaths and take a statement of truth. When meeting a client, a notary will request evidence of identity (passport or the like) and will need to be satisfied that the person understands any document, particularly a document that is not in English. The Notaries Society is the representative society for the 900 or so notaries public practising in England and Wales. The rules that affect notaries are very similar to the rules that affect solicitors. However, in addition to qualifying as a solicitor or barrister, a candidate seeking to qualify as a notary public will need to study Roman/civil law, conflicts of law and notarial practice.

(d) 'Legal executive' – Many firms employ staff who are not admitted to the legal profession in order to assist with the routine work of a legal office, such as conveyancing or preparing accounts. Previously, such staff were known as managing clerks. However, legal executives now have a profession that is governed by the Institute of Legal Executives (ILEX), which prescribes examinations and regulations for admission to its ranks. Legal executives have a right of audience in chambers (i.e. not in open court) and a limited right of audience in open court in the county court.

(e) 'Licensed conveyancer' – Until the mid–1980s solicitors and barristers were the only people who could undertake conveyancing work (although barristers were almost never involved). Drawing up a conveyance involves preparing documents relating to the transfer of title to property for gain. The new profession of licensed conveyancers was created by Part II of the **Administration of Justice Act 1985** in order to open up the work to competition and reduce the fees payable by the public. The new profession is governed by the Council for Licensed Conveyancers.

Common Pitfalls ✘

Students are usually happy to see such a question for in their eyes it is an easy question. The issue in choosing such a question to answer in an exam is that it may be an easy question to pass, but it will be difficult to get the top marks without a very comprehensive and accurate answer.

Aim Higher ★

Add value to your answer by giving as much detail as possible regarding the particular role of the branch of the legal profession. This is the way to garner as many marks as possible.

QUESTION 14

Many people are deterred from seeking legal advice and taking legal action because they fear having to pay high legal fees. What schemes and organisations exist to provide low-cost legal help, and are they available to commercial organisations?

Answer Plan

❖   Provide background information arising as a result of the **Access to Justice Act 1999**.

❖   Discuss the Community Legal Service Fund (also known as Legal Aid), which provides community legal services and a criminal defence service.

❖   Discuss the new conditional fee arrangement system introduced by the **Courts and Legal Services Act 1990**.

ANSWER

The Community Service Legal Fund (also known as Legal Aid) helps people who cannot afford legal services, as long as they meet certain conditions. The fund was established by the **Access to Justice Act 1999** and is administered by the Legal Services Commission.

Unlike commercial clients, who are not able to access the fund, private individuals may be able to obtain financial assistance in certain civil legal matters. Civil legal matters that fall within the scope of the new scheme include such matters as housing, welfare benefits and financial claims, credit and debts, contractual disputes, clinical negligence or claims arising from divorce. Certain types of problems are not covered by the scheme, namely, neighbour or boundary disputes, conveyancing (i.e. transfer of land title), company or partnership law, defamation and malicious falsehood. Applicants are eligible for Legal Aid if they receive certain state benefits or are on a low income. The applicant must apply to the Community Legal Fund and if the application is successful, the solicitor will be authorised to carry out two hours of work or three hours in a family law case. If additional legal services are required from the solicitor, the solicitor must apply to the Legal Services Commission for permission to continue to act for the legally-aided client. The decision will be determined on the basis of whether the client's case has merit and justifies further legal support. If court proceedings are required, the solicitor will need to obtain a Legal Representation Certificate from the Commission.

In relation to criminal matters, the **Access to Justice Act 1999** states that advice, assistance and representation in criminal law matters are provided by private solicitors and public defenders who are engaged by the Legal Services Commission for this purpose. Duty solicitors are on hand in magistrates' courts and police stations to provide legal advice. The Citizens' Advice Bureau also provides free legal advice and assistance to private individuals. Many inner-city areas also have voluntary Law Centres.

In terms of legal fees, solicitors charge in different ways, including hourly rates, fixed fees and percentage fees. At the start of the case, the solicitor explains the likely cost of the case and how the charge is calculated. Since 1998, a conditional fee agreement is now also possible between a client (whether a private client or a commercial client) and a solicitor for all civil matters except family proceedings or criminal matters. This type of agreement is commonly known as 'no win, no fee'. This method of funding legal services was introduced by the **Courts and Legal Services Act 1990**.

In a 'no win, no fee' agreement, the solicitor will only be paid if the claim is successful. The solicitor will also be entitled to an extra fee plus an 'uplift' in the event of success, called a 'success' fee. The percentage of any success fee must be set out in the agreement and can be no higher than 100 per cent.

Both the basic fee and the success fee are usually paid in whole or partly by the losing party. Other legal costs may include court fees or a fee for an expert report, for example, and these are called 'disbursements'. Similarly, the losing party should pay all or part of these disbursements as well. However, the client is still liable to pay the solicitor for any costs that the losing party is not ordered to pay.

If the claim fails, the client will not have to pay his own solicitor, but will still have to pay the costs of the successful party, including disbursements, if ordered to do so. However, as part of the conditional fee agreement, the solicitor will usually have arranged legal insurance to cover this risk. This is known as 'after the event' insurance and the client will simply be asked to pay the premium. For a 'no win, no fee' arrangement to be valid, the solicitor must ensure that the legal formalities have been complied with.

The 'no win, no fee' method of funding legal actions is increasingly relied on by private clients and in some cases, commercial clients, to assist them to fund legal actions.

Common Pitfalls

A failure to refer to the particular legislation that is the authority for the various schemes will result in a reduction in the marks awarded.

Aim Higher

Aim to demonstrate your practical knowledge of both the way in which legal fees are charged and the range of options for securing payment of legal fees.

Alternative Dispute Resolution

INTRODUCTION

Legal problems are likely to arise in the course of any business, especially in the performance of all but the most straightforward contracts. It is good practice to agree how to deal with problems during the negotiation phase, rather than when the legal problem has arisen and the formerly cordial business relationship has started to break down.

It is important not to let legal rights get in the way of finding a solution. Establishing legal liability can be costly in both time and money. Most problems are resolved by negotiation between the parties without the need to resort to litigation in court. The alternatives to litigation are usually referred to as 'alternative dispute resolution' (ADR). If the parties cannot resolve their dispute themselves, they can agree to use one of several forms of alternative dispute resolution to seek to resolve it. Indeed, the court's Civil Procedure Rules now require courts to encourage parties to use ADR to resolve their disputes in appropriate cases.

The term ADR covers several different processes for dispute resolution without the involvement of the court system. Each type of ADR has different characteristics, resulting in advantages and disadvantages if a particular method is adopted. Key forms of ADR include:

❖ Arbitration (governed by the **Arbitration Act 1996**);
❖ Early neutral evaluation (by a lawyer or an expert);
❖ Expert determination (an independent expert decides the outcome);
❖ Mediation (use of a neutral third party to either 'evaluate' or 'facilitate' a resolution);
❖ Conciliation (a neutral third party helps the parties to reach agreement).

QUESTION 15

Your IT business has a dispute over a technology contract with an important, long-standing client. The dispute arose shortly after the acceptance testing of the new technology. You wish to consider mediation in order to settle the claim and avoid court. Consider if mediation would be an appropriate alternative dispute resolution (ADR) technique in this instance.

Answer Plan

This is a practical problem question which asks the student to critically analyse mediation as a form of ADR with the aim of retaining a long-standing commercial client.

❖   Introduce the considerations relevant to a technology contract dispute and the long-standing business relationship.
❖   Briefly explain how mediation works and its advantages and disadvantages.
❖   Consider the option of expert determination by contract.

ANSWER

Technology contracts often contemplate a long-term relationship because the supplier will not get the expected return on the transaction if the deal falls apart during acceptance testing, and the buyer will be left high and dry. Unfortunately, litigious procedures are not designed to salvage such a situation because the mandatory court documentation and procedures are slow and costly.

It is important for the IT business to avoid initiating litigation, as it would result in their client immediately becoming an adversary. Invariably the business relationship will be damaged, if not irreparably lost. In addition, litigation necessarily requires the involvement of key business staff, which takes their time and energy away from other productive pursuits. These resources will not be recovered by way of damages or reimbursement, even if the IT company were to be successful. Furthermore, legal proceedings invariably take several months, if not years, to finalise. This is not only due to the courts' management of the case, which has improved recently, but due to the fact that lawyers are very clever at using the law to defeat the law. A skilled lawyer is able to prolong a case.

While some forms of ADR are more common than others, there is really no set format. ADR techniques can be mixed and matched to suit the circumstances, which is one of their strengths. And, even if the parties choose litigation, this can still be combined with certain forms of ADR; in particular, mediation. In this case, the lawyers and judges may be unfamiliar with the terminology and technological concepts involved, which also suggests that mediation would be an especially appropriate method of dispute resolution in this instance.

Mediation would work in the present case for several reasons. Essentially, a third party whom the parties have accepted as a mediator will receive written statements from the parties. The mediator is usually trained in techniques designed to assist people to find solutions to their problems. The mediator structuring the negotiations between the parties may impose a solution or decision or simply facilitate the discussion. A mediator does not make a decision or an award.

The reasons why resolving a dispute using mediation is effective are:

❖ the parties' negotiation skills may have broken down as they are not trained in negotiation skills – mediators are;

❖ parties are more likely to moderate their behaviour in the presence of an impartial third person;

❖ while the mediator does not impose solutions on the parties, the mediator can suggest solutions for the parties to think about. Parties are more willing to accept suggestions from an impartial third person than from the 'other side';

❖ unlike more formal procedures, which may focus on the parties' legal rights, mediation can focus on the interests the parties need to see addressed before they can reach a negotiated resolution.

The mediation process begins when the parties choose the mediator and the procedures they will follow during the mediation. The mediator's role is to control the process, to restrain the parties from going off track and to guide the parties to the track suitable to them. Mediation can be very informal and limited to a few people, or rather more structured, with each party attending meetings with its lawyers. The parties control the outcome, be it successful or not. At the end of a successful mediation, the parties record their agreement in writing and it is enforced as a contract between them.

Another form of ADR may also be appropriate and should be considered by the IT business; this is known as 'expert determination' by contract. Many disputes in technology contracts arise in relation to the customer's perception of unsatisfactory performance of the technology. Expert determination is ideally suited to these disputes and requires the expert to make a decision that is binding on the parties. As long as the parties can agree on an expert, this person can determine the disputed facts by evaluating the parties' claims and seeking or clarifying information s/he considers relevant to the dispute. For example, have the acceptance tests been passed or should a certificate of acceptance be issued? This avoids complex technical issues being decided by judges unversed in their complexities. The process involves:

❖ appointment of the expert;
❖ submission of the issue(s) to be determined;
❖ submissions by each party;
❖ questions by the expert;
❖ delivery of the expert's determination.

It is important to note that an expert determination does not determine legal rights; the expert is supposed to make his determination based on experience, not the persuasions of a party or the law. Effectively, the expert's determination can affect legal rights, for example, if the determination decides the price of a technical change or whether a system meets the technical specifications. Expert determinations are not able to be appealed against unless the parties have agreed on an appeal process. If a party fails to accept the expert's determination, they can be sued for breach of contract. Given the existence of a contract between the parties, the expert owes a duty of care to the parties and can be sued in negligence if his award is affected by negligence.

If the dispute can be settled amicably, either through mediation or expert determination, it is highly likely that the parties will be able to continue to do business with each other.

Common Pitfalls ✖

Several forms of ADR need to be discussed for a complete answer, which allows little scope for lengthy discussion of any one issue. After general introductory comments regarding ADR, begin to evaluate the best options for the IT business.

Aim Higher ★

Reach a conclusion on the preferred option(s) for the IT business in terms of resolving their problem, taking into account the nature of the IT business and the essence of the dispute and any other relevant facts in the scenario.

QUESTION 16

Compare and contrast arbitration, mediation and conciliation as alternatives to litigation in court, noting the pros and cons of each. When is ADR not appropriate?

Answer Plan

This question requires the student to demonstrate knowledge of three different forms of ADR and provide an analysis of the circumstances in which ADR is best avoided. Apart from describing each form of ADR, in order to attract higher marks the student should evaluate the merits of each.

❖   Introduce the need for ADR and the disadvantages of litigation in general.
❖   Discuss arbitration, mediation and conciliation in turn.
❖   Consider the circumstances in which ADR is not appropriate, such as when an injunction is required, when the dispute relates to a debt only, or when the law is unclear and requires a court ruling.

ANSWER

Litigation should always be the last resort for a business because it is so costly, time-consuming and complex. If the case is lost, the loser will have to pay not only his own legal costs, but also the costs of the other party. Even if the case is won, full legal costs are not always recovered. There is also the financial risk, particularly when the case concerns securing the payment of a debt, that the other side will become insolvent and not pay. Another reason to avoid litigation and consider ADR is that litigation creates lasting ill-feeling. If a business sues a customer then wins or loses, this is likely to be the end of the business relationship. If the dispute can be settled amicably, the parties may continue to do business with each other. As litigation takes place in open court, the dispute becomes public, which may generate negative publicity. Alternative dispute resolution can avoid this bad publicity.

There are three main types of ADR: arbitration, mediation and conciliation.

'Arbitration' is the process in which disputes are resolved by an independent arbitrator rather than by a court. A dispute may be referred to arbitration by the parties themselves, by a term of a contract between the parties, by a court or by an Act of Parliament. In arbitration, lawyers can still represent the parties, and the rules of procedure are similar to litigation. Proceedings might not be much cheaper than litigation, but will probably be speedier. The arbitrator's decision is binding on the parties. The **Arbitration Act 1996** consolidates the law on arbitration. The legislation provides that the arbitrator should act fairly and impartially between the parties, giving each party a reasonable opportunity of putting his/her case and dealing with that of the opponent. A party can apply for a stay of proceedings if the other party brings court proceedings in respect of a matter that it has been agreed should be resolved by arbitration. A disadvantage of arbitration is that it is an increasingly lengthy and expensive process, albeit less so than litigation.

In 'mediation', the parties themselves agree the resolution of the dispute. The mediator's role is to try to facilitate such an agreement. There are no fixed rules as to how mediation might operate. Generally, the parties would first present an outline of their case to each other, in the presence of the mediator, and reply to the other party's case. The mediator will set out the rules, trying to keep matters simple and striving to identify the key issues in dispute. Then the two or more sides will probably repair to different rooms and the mediator will spend time with one group, before passing on the position of that party to the other party or parties. The mediator will attempt to identify the strengths and weaknesses of each party's arguments to bring the parties to mutual agreement. However, the mediator has no power to enforce the agreement. A disadvantage may be that not all parties taking part in the mediation are genuinely attempting to settle the case. They might merely be trying to find out the strengths and weaknesses of the other party's case.

'Conciliation' is similar to mediation, except that the conciliator actually suggests a basis for settlement to the parties. However, the conciliator's recommendation is not binding on the parties.

By and large, business people do not like to hold grudges because it is not in their interest and so they are keen to consider ADR options. However, at times, ADR fails or is inappropriate. Even where ADR fails, however, it is likely that the parties will have narrowed the scope of their dispute, or clarified the issues, so that litigation may be speedier or less costly than it otherwise would have been; consequently, ADR is unlikely to be a complete waste of money. However, ADR is inappropriate in the following situations:

(1) When an injunction is required. An injunction is an order by which a party to an action is required to do, or refrain from doing, something;
(2) Where there is no dispute between the parties, for example where a debt is owed;
(3) Where the law is unclear so that a ruling by a court is required.

In conclusion, although litigation is not a panacea, sometimes it is the only alternative if the parties are unable to negotiate a satisfactory resolution to their problem.

Common Pitfalls ✖

Throughout your academic career, you'll be asked to write papers in which you compare and contrast things. You may feel daunted by a list of seemingly unrelated similarities and differences, or confused about how to construct a paper that isn't just a mechanical exercise in which you first state all the features that A and B have in common, and then state all the ways in which A and B are different. The best approach is thinking about the *grounds for comparison*, i.e. the rationale behind your choice. This lets the examiner know why your choice is deliberate and meaningful, not random.

Aim Higher ★

Remember the final question – when is ADR not appropriate? Within the structure of your answer, the answer to this question should be dealt with toward the end of your essay, in line with the structure of the question.

QUESTION 17 --

Can legal costs be recovered by the successful party in a civil court action and, second, what issues should be taken into account when making a cost–benefit analysis of whether to begin legal proceedings in court in the first place?

Answer Plan

This is basically a two-part essay question involving: (1) recovery of legal costs and disbursements in legal proceedings; and (2) an explanation of the practical steps used to evaluate whether it is in a business's interest to begin or settle litigation.

 ❖ Discuss recovery of costs and disbursement in civil legal proceedings and the principle that the losing party will normally be ordered to pay all or a proportion of the winner's costs.
 ❖ Consider the nature of the court's discretion to make a costs award and the factors the court takes into account when assessing entitlement to costs.
 ❖ Explain the factors to be considered in deciding whether to bring or settle a civil legal action.

ANSWER

In most civil litigation, each party is responsible for paying its own legal fees unless a costs award is made in their favour. The rules relating to the payment and recovery of legal costs and disbursements in legal proceedings come into play and those contemplating launching litigation should be aware of these. In particular, claimants need to understand their chances of being awarded costs before they take legal action to enforce their rights, especially to avoid unpleasant shocks further down the legal line.

RECOVERY OF COSTS – IF THE CLAIM IS SUCCESSFUL

Save for 'small claims' cases, where costs awards are usually minimal, the losing party at a hearing or trial or otherwise will normally be ordered to pay all or a proportion of the winner's legal costs. The court has full discretion as to what costs order to make in terms of both entitlement and amount. Factors that may be taken into account by the court in assessing entitlement to and/or the amount of costs to be awarded include the following:

(1) the track (if any) to which the claim has been allocated, that is, the fast track or multi-track (which will usually depend on the value of the claim);

(2) whether the amount of costs claimed is proportionate and/or reasonable and necessary to the matters in issue and/or the value of the claim;

(3) the conduct of the parties both before and during the proceedings. Conduct can include:

    (a) whether it was reasonable for a party to raise, pursue or contest a particular allegation or issue;

    (b) the manner in which a party has pursued or defended a claim; and

    (c) whether or not a party exaggerated his or her claim.

(4) attempts at settlement. For example, even if a party is successful at trial, it may be deprived of all or a proportion of its costs if it has refused to take part in mediation;

(5) success in whole or in part; and

(6) the value and complexity of the case, specialist knowledge involved, time spent and place of performance.

In light of the court's discretion to award and assess legal costs, there is no guarantee that a successful party can expect an order against the losing party for any specified or minimum portion of the costs.

COST–BENEFIT ANALYSIS OF A CIVIL ACTION

The choice of whether to bring or defend a civil legal action in court should be carefully analysed, just as with any other important business decision. This includes performing a cost–benefit analysis of the merits of the case. For the claimant, it may be wise not to sue. For the defendant, it may be wise to settle. The following factors should be considered when deciding whether to bring or settle a civil legal action:

- ❖ the probability of winning or losing – this will usually involve getting a legal opinion;
- ❖ the amount of money to be won or lost (the amount of the claim);
- ❖ an estimate of lawyers' fees and other costs of the litigation (e.g. expert fees, photographs);
- ❖ the loss of time by managers and other staff who assist to prepare the case;
- ❖ the long-term effects on the relationship and reputation of the parties as a hearing or trial is open to the public and may be the subject of news reports;
- ❖ the aggravation and psychological costs associated with being involved in a stressful court case that may have strict deadlines;
- ❖ the unpredictability of the legal system and the possibility of error and/or the need to appeal;
- ❖ other factors peculiar to the parties and the lawsuit.

If a claimant nevertheless wishes to proceed with court action, there are four practical considerations that need to be determined:

(1) Identify the key issues and events to be achieved as a result of the litigation.
(2) Identify any commercial considerations relevant to the dispute.
(3) Identify who will manage the dispute and provide instructions to the solicitors.
(4) Identify the relevant witnesses including current and former employees.

At any time in the litigation process, before proceedings have begun or after, it may be appropriate for either party to consider making an offer to settle. Litigation is expensive and time-consuming and the parties should always bear in mind the cost–benefit analysis of continuing with the litigation. The parties should try to take a commercial view as to the costs of persevering with litigation. An offer can be made informally or formally in accordance with the rules of the court. A formal offer (called a Part 36 Civil Procedure Rules 1998 offer) has cost consequences, which can be considered as a matter of strategy.

In conclusion, a decision to take legal action should not be taken lightly as legal proceedings can be costly, lengthy and very stressful to the individual or to a firm.

Common Pitfalls ✘

The question demands that the student should think commercially about the nature of litigation and when it is in a claimant's interest to begin legal proceedings. Therefore, your answer should be appropriately balanced between the various issues.

Aim Higher ★

Examiners will be looking for a discussion of a variety of factors that a party should take into account when determining to begin legal proceedings, with a particular focus on recovery of legal costs for the successful claimant.

European Community Law and Human Rights

INTRODUCTION

In 1973, the United Kingdom (UK) joined the European Economic Community (now the European Union (EU)) when it signed the original EEC treaty – the Treaty of Rome. As a condition of membership, the UK was required to pass the **European Communities Act 1972**, which had two consequences. First, the UK must apply EU law in its courts and second, if there is a conflict between EU law and UK domestic law, then the EU law will prevail. This means that UK legislation must be interpreted in a way that is consistent with EU law.

Four key European institutions form the framework for the system of EU law. These are the Council of European Communities ('the Council'), the European Commission, the European Parliament and the European Court of Justice.

There are three sources of EU law:

1. law enacted by Member States, which are the founding treaties (primary legislation) and law enacted by the European Commission (secondary legislation);
2. general principles of law recognised by the European Court of Justice (ECJ); and
3. international agreement with non-Member States.

The secondary legislation of the EU exists in three types of rules:

1. Regulations that are 'directly applicable' in all Member States;
2. Directives that are not immediately binding and require Member States to pass domestic legislation; and
3. Decisions that are immediately binding on those to whom they are addressed.

If EU legislation is directly applicable it automatically becomes law in the Member States. However, no EU legislation can have 'direct effect' unless it is sufficiently clear, precise and unconditional. If EU legislation has direct vertical effect it can be used by an individual only against the State and against emanations of the State, such as public authorities. If the EU legislation has direct horizontal effect, it can be used by one individual against another.

Every Member State is a signatory of the **European Convention on Human Rights 1950**. The UK ratified this Convention in 1951, but did not pass domestic legislation so that human rights could be directly enforced in UK courts until it enacted the **Human Rights Act 1998 (HRA)**. **Section 2** of the **HRA** requires any court or tribunal that is considering a question related to a Convention right to take into account any relevant decision of the ECJ. **Section 3** of the **HRA** requires that all legislation be read and given effect in a way that is compatible with Convention rights to the greatest extent possible. A UK precedent-making court has the authority to make a declaration of incompatibility, stating that legislation is incompatible with Convention rights. If this happens, the relevant minister can revoke, amend or leave the incompatible UK legislation in place. All courts can declare delegated legislation invalid on the ground of incompatibility with Convention rights. **Section 6(1)** of the **HRA** states that it is unlawful for a public authority to act in a way that is inconsistent with a Convention right, unless the public authority could not have acted in any other way, due to the provision of a UK statute. This section, in effect, creates a new public tort.

The human rights enshrined in the **Convention on Human Rights** are as follows:

1. **Article 2** – The right to life;
2. **Article 3** – The right not to be subjected to torture or inhuman treatment or degrading punishment;
3. **Article 4** – The right not to be held in slavery or servitude or required to perform forced or compulsory labour;
4. **Article 5** – The right to liberty and security of the person;
5. **Article 6** – The right to a fair trial;
6. **Article 7** – The right not to be convicted of a criminal offence which was created after the act was committed;
7. **Article 8** – The right to respect for a person's private and family life, home and correspondence;
8. **Article 9** – The right to freedom of thought, conscience and religion;
9. **Article 10** – The right to freedom of expression;
10. **Article 11** – The right to freedom of peaceful assembly and freedom of association with others;
11. **Article 12** – The right to marry and form a family;
12. **Article 14** – The right to have the Convention applied without discrimination.

Note that **Articles 1** and **13** have not been incorporated into UK domestic law. The UK is also bound by **Protocol 1**, which gives the right to peaceful enjoyment of property and possessions, the right to education and the right to free elections. **Protocol 6** outlaws the death penalty.

The European Commission on Human Rights ensures that a petition to the European Court of Human Rights (ECHR) is admissible and tries to help the parties to resolve a dispute. The ECHR sits in Strasbourg and adjudicates on petitions brought by individual citizens against a State and cases brought by one State against another.

Finally, in Nice in December 2000, the European Union Charter of Fundamental Rights was agreed by the Presidents of Council, EU Commission and Parliament to cover additional matters outside the scope of the Convention (e.g. economic and social rights).

QUESTION 18

Explain the origin, composition, role and function of the European Court of Justice as well as its status within the English legal system.

Answer Plan

This essay question calls for the student to clearly answer on five issues in relation to the ECJ. Although it is not strictly a subdivided question, markers will be looking for evidence that the student has comprehensively dealt with each of the five aspects in his or her essay.

1. Initially set out details of how the ECJ came into existence.
2. Next, cover the judicial personnel involved and their term of appointment.
3. Discuss the ECJ's jurisdiction and its role to adjudicate cases referred to it by a General Court or a national court.
4. Clarify the decision-making processes and procedures used by the ECJ.
5. Explain the status of the ECJ in terms of judicial precedent in the English legal system.

ANSWER

The European Court of Justice (ECJ) was set up under the Treaty of Rome to give rulings on questions of law relating to the interpretation and application of the Treaty. The ECJ sits in Luxembourg and is made up of 27 judges. The judges and advocates are appointed by common consent of the Member States and hold office for a six-year term which may be renewed. The decision of the court are signed by all the judges, without any indication that some may have dissented. The ECJ exercises judicial power within the European Community. Its jurisdiction covers:

(a) Preliminary rulings concerning the interpretation of the treaty or community legislation enacted under the treaty;
(b) Actions against Member States;
(c) Actions against Community institutions; and
(d) Community employment cases.

The Court is composed of the 27 judges, one from each member state of the EU, as well as several Advocates General, whose role is to assist the judges. It is intended that a judge will draw on the legal tradition of his particular Member State rather than represent the Member State itself. There are an uneven number of judges so as always to have a majority decision. All judges sign the decision and there is no disclosure of which judges have dissented with the majority. Interestingly, an Advocate General has the same status as a judge and his duty is to present an impartial and reasoned opinion on the case, before the judges' deliberations. The Advocate General is completely independent and does not represent a particular interest, but s/he hopes to influence the Court through his or her presentation. The ECJ does not adopt a system of judicial precedent and can depart from its own decisions.

The function of the ECJ is to ensure that, in the interpretation and application of the Treaty, the law is observed. However, as the caseload of the ECJ has increased, the time to receive an ECJ judgment can take up to two years. In order to reduce the ECJ's workload, the General Court (EGC) (known until late 2009 as the Court of First Instance (CFI)) was created by the **Single European Act** in **1986**. CFIs began to hear cases in 1989. It is possible to appeal a General Court decision to the ECJ on points of law on three grounds:

(1) Lack of competence of the EGC;
(2) Breach of procedure before the EGC, which adversely affects the interests of the applicant; and
(3) Infringement of Community law by the EGC.

The ECJ may also be referred cases from a national court, which can request an authoritative ruling on the interpretation of any EU legislation.

In relation to the English legal system, the Supreme Court must seek a preliminary ruling from the ECJ where a point of EU law is ambiguous or otherwise at issue and the ECJ had not previously interpreted the point. The principle of supremacy was established in *Costa v ENEL* (1964) and provides that, where national law and EC law conflict, then the EC law shall prevail. Finally, since joining the EU in 1973, all English courts have been bound by decisions of the ECJ in matters of European law.

QUESTION 19

Explain the differences between the following pairs of legal terminology:

(1) European Community and the European Union;
(2) A Regulation and a Directive;
(3) The **European Convention on Human Rights** and the **European Union Charter of Fundamental Rights**.

Answer Plan

This is a subdivided question requiring the student to demonstrate general knowledge and understanding. Answer (1) and (3) in turn, clearly identifying each section by number. Unless you are told otherwise, it is reasonable for you to assume that each section carries equal marks. This means that each section is worth 33⅓ per cent and you should allocate equal time to each subsection.

ANSWER

(1) 'European Community and the European Union' – Since the **Treaty on European Union 1991 (TEU)** was ratified it is more common to use the term European Union (EU). The EU comprises several EU communities including:
   ❖ European Community (formerly known as the European Economic Community);
   ❖ European Coal and Steel Community;
   ❖ European Atomic Energy Community;

❖ Intergovernmental cooperation on foreign affairs and security policy (CFSP), justice and home affairs.

Action relating to the CFSP, justice and home affairs takes place by way of intergovernmental cooperation and the ECJ has no jurisdiction.

(2) 'A Regulation and a Directive' – Both Regulations and Directives are secondary EU legislation created by the Council, acting with the European Parliament, or by the European Commission. Regulations are directly applicable in all Member States without the approval of the Parliaments of those States. The UK Parliament cannot pass an Act that conflicts with an EU Regulation. Regulations deal with technical issues such as which colourings can be added to food. Directives, on the other hand, are not immediately binding, but require Member States to pass legislation to bring them into effect by the implementation date. The UK usually implements Directives by delegated legislation, but it may also pass primary legislation, for example a statute, if necessary.

(3) '**European Convention on Human Rights (ECHR)** and the **European Union Charter of Fundamental Rights (the Charter)**' – In 1950, the Council of Europe adopted the **ECHR**, which was based on the United Nations' Universal Declaration on Human Rights. The UK ratified the **ECHR** in 1951. The **ECHR** provides three types of Convention rights: absolute rights, limited rights and qualified rights. The **ECHR** also established the European Court of Human Rights and procedures to protect the Convention rights. Convention rights include the right to life, freedom from inhuman treatment, freedom from slavery, right to liberty, right to a fair trial, protection against retrospective claims, right to private and family life, freedom of conscience, freedom of expression, freedom of assembly and association, right to marry and freedom from discrimination. The **Charter** came into existence in 2000 and its articles extend beyond the scope of the **ECHR** to cover economic and social rights (e.g. right to vote, right to health care, right to fair and just working conditions, among others).

Common Pitfalls ✘

Comprehension cannot be shown without knowledge. This question requires the student to demonstrate both knowledge and comprehension.

Aim Higher ★

Ensure you have defined and explained each term accurately before going on to discuss the topic in more depth.

QUESTION 20

What different forms of European legislation are there, and what is meant by 'direct applicability' and 'direct effect'?

Answer Plan

There are three key issues to be covered in this essay question, namely:

(1)   Forms of EU legislation;
(2)   The meaning of 'direct applicability'; and
(3)   The meaning of 'direct effect'.

With respect to direct effect, a good answer will explain the difference between vertical and horizontal direct effect. In addition, by way of contrast, an explanation of the term 'indirect effect', illustrated and supported by the ECJ decision in *Van Gend en Loos v Nederlandse Administratie der Belastingen* (1963), should also be discussed.

ANSWER

The amended Treaty of Rome now contains over 300 articles of law and these articles make up the primary legislation of the EU. There are three types of secondary EU legislation that are created by the Council acting with the European Parliament or by the Commission. The three types of secondary legislation include Regulations, Directives and legal decisions.

An important issue in relation to European Union law principles is applicability and effect. In order to understand the effect of EU law, it is necessary to understand the distinction between the terms 'direct applicability' and 'direct effect'. Direct applicability is when EU law is passed into the national courts without the Member State having to implement the law. Treaty Articles and Regulations have direct application and do not need to be implemented by Member States.

However, in order for individuals to invoke the Articles or Regulations in either a cause of action in court or a defence to a court action, the ECJ developed the doctrine of 'direct effect'. This doctrine enables an individual citizen to enforce Community rights derived from the treaties in domestic courts. The position is that Articles and Regulations can only have direct effect if they meet the criteria set out in the ECJ's decision in the case of *Van Gend en Loos v Nederlandse Administratie der Belastingen* (1963). It was held that the provisions must be clear and unconditional. Once they satisfy these requirements they can have direct effect. If they do not satisfy the criteria they can have indirect effect.

Direct effect can be direct vertical effect or direct horizontal effect. If EU legislation has direct vertical effect it can be used by an individual only against the State and against emanations of the State, such as public authorities, for example a health authority. If the EU legislation has direct horizontal effect, it can be used by one individual against another.

Directives seek to harmonise the law of the Member States. They function as instructions to Member States to bring their laws into line by a certain date. Directives, unlike Regulations, do not have direct applicability and it is up to the Member States to implement them in a way that suits their political and economic culture. Implementation in the UK might, for example, take the form of an Act of Parliament or a statutory instrument. English law usually implements EC Directives through delegated legislation.

As mentioned earlier, Directives have an implementation date and if they are not implemented by that date, the Commission will take proceedings against that Member State for failure to implement the Directives. The Directives can also have 'direct effect' if they meet the ECJ's *Van Gend en Loos v Nederlandse Administratie der Belastingen* (1963) criteria. These criteria will be satisfied only if the legislation is sufficiently clear, precise and unconditional, and if the legislation intends to confer rights. Many articles do not meet these criteria as they are mere statements of aspiration. If a Directive does not meet the *Van Gend* criteria, then they will have indirect effect. The ECJ developed the concept of 'indirect effect' of Directives by requiring national courts to interpret national law in light of the wording and purpose of a Directive to achieve the result intended by the Directive: *Von Colson and Kamann v Land Nordrhein-Westfalen* (1984).

Common Pitfalls ✗

To answer this question, it is best to adopt the precise terminology of European Union law for the sake of clarity rather than to try to express it in other terms.

Aim Higher ★

Highlight the key ECJ case *Van Gend en Loos*, which held that no EU legislation can have direct effect unless it is sufficiently clear, precise and unconditional.

Comparative Legal Systems
6 Civil Law, US Law, Japanese Law, People's Republic Of China, *Sharia* and Hindu Law

INTRODUCTION

Business transcends borders and therefore it is important to have an awareness of the legal frameworks of key foreign trade markets such as the USA, Japan and China as well as the world's important religious-based legal traditions, such as *Sharia* and Hindu.

THE EUROPEAN (ROMANO-GERMAN) CIVIL LAW SYSTEM

Now that the United Kingdom is part of the European Union it is important to develop an understanding of the European civil law system. The civil law system is the most widespread legal system in the world. It derives from 450 BC when Rome adopted the Twelve Tables, a code of laws applicable to Roman citizens. A compilation of Roman law, called the *Corpus Juris Civilis* (the Body of Civil Law), was completed in AD 534. Later, two national codes, the French Civil Code of 1804 (the Napoleonic Code) and the German Civil Code of 1896, became the preferred models for countries that sought to adopt civil codes. In contrast to the English legal system, where laws are created by legislation as well as the judicial system, the European Civil Code and parliamentary statutes that expand and interpret them are the sole sources of law in most civil law countries. This means that, when a case is adjudicated in court, it is a matter of applying the relevant code provisions to the particular fact situation.

THE UNITED STATES' ANGLO-AMERICAN LEGAL SYSTEM

The USA is Britain's largest single export market, taking £33.3 billion of UK goods in 2010 (14.3 per cent of the UK's exports). The UK is the sixth biggest exporter to the USA, after Canada, Mexico, China, Japan and Germany. The USA is also the leading overseas destination for British investment. In terms of law, the Constitution of the United States of America is the supreme law of the country. Any law, whether federal, state or local, which conflicts with the US Constitution is unlawful and unconstitutional and not enforceable. The principles set out in the US Constitution are very broad, because the authors of the document intended them to be able to be applied to future social, technological and economic developments. The US Constitution created three arms of government and gave them powers as follows:

❖ Legislative (Congress), which has the power to enact law;
❖ Executive (President), which has the power to enforce the law;
❖ Judicial (Courts), which has the power to interpret and determine the validity of the law.

As this is a federal system, powers not given to the federal government by the Constitution are reserved for the states that also have their own constitutions. State constitutions establish the three arms of state government and their powers in a similar fashion. Provisions of state constitutions are valid unless they conflict with the US Constitution or any valid federal law.

In relation to business, the US Congress is empowered by the Commerce Clause in the US Constitution to enact federal statutes to regulate foreign and interstate commerce. Federal statutes include antitrust (competition), securities laws, bankruptcy, labour (employment), environmental protection and consumer protection laws.

The Executive branch of the government, which includes the President of the United States and state governors, is empowered to issue executive orders. For example, when the United States is at war with another country, the US President usually issues executive orders prohibiting US companies from selling goods or services to that country.

Federal and state courts issue judicial decisions setting out their legal reasoning for deciding the case. These decisions often include interpretations of statutes. As the USA is historically a former colony of England, the judicial systems are very similar in that past court decisions become precedent for deciding future cases. Lower courts must follow the precedent established by higher courts and all courts must follow precedents made by the US Supreme Court.

THE JAPANESE LEGAL TRADITION

Japan is the UK's largest export market outside Europe and the USA. It represents 12 per cent of world's gross domestic product (GDP) and took £3.68 billion of UK goods and services in 2009. After a long sluggish period following the economic problems of the early 1990s, the Japanese economy has started showing signs of recovery, with GDP growing by 2.7 per cent in 2006, and corporate Japan returning record profits. Japan is a sophisticated, competitive and stable business market for British exporters and investors. British exports to Japan grew by 2.8 per cent in 2005 to £3,700 million. Exports were dominated by three major sectors: chemical products, machinery and transport equipment. The Japanese market has undergone much deregulation over the past 20 years and is now relatively open in most sectors.

Historically, Japanese law was influenced by Chinese law and then developed independently during the Edo period through texts such as the *Kujikata Osadamegaki*. However, since the late nineteenth century the Japanese legal system has been largely based on the civil law of Germany.

Japan's legislature, the National Diet of Japan, enacts laws with the approval of the Emperor as a formality. The main body of Japanese law originates with the Six Codes, which are the: (1) Constitution of Japan; (2) Civil Code; (3) Criminal Code; (4) Commercial Code; (5) Code of Civil Procedure; and (6) Code of Criminal Procedure.

As Japan has a civil law system, judicial decisions are not binding on lower courts. However, the precedents of the Japanese Supreme Court and the High Courts are regularly cited and are persuasive.

JAPANESE CONTRACT LAW

Japanese contract law is codified and defines the rights and obligations of the parties generally. Practically speaking, Japanese contracts are terse and tend to contain very little detail with the parties negotiating complications as they arise.

In Japan (as well as China and other Asian countries), individuals often do not use their hand-applied signatures to sign legal documents. Instead, they follow the ancient tradition of using a stamp as their signature. The stamp is a character or set of characters carved onto the end of a cylinder-shaped piece made of ivory, jade, agate, gold, animal horn, wood or even plastic, and is designed to be held in a person's hand. The imprint made with ink serves as the owner's signature. In Japan, the cylinder is called a *hanko* and in China it is called a *chop*. Hankos and chops are registered with the government.

In the UK, where use of personal signatures is the norm, if a signature is suspected of being a forgery, there is a great deal of forensic technology that can now be used to prove it is not a legitimate signature. However, in Japan, where stamps are used, it is much more difficult to detect and prove a forgery because anyone who gains access to the stamp can apply it. It is thought that the use of stamps is on the decline, especially as the younger generation increasingly adopts the use of signatures.

LITIGATION IN JAPAN

In terms of its legal tradition, Japan adheres to the attitude that confrontation should be avoided. Japan is a much less litigious country than, say, the United States and it only has about one-fiftieth of the lawyers that the USA has. No class action or contingency fee arrangements are permitted in Japan. Claimants must pay their lawyers an upfront fee of up to 8 per cent of the compensation sought, plus a non-refundable court filing fee of one-half of 1 per cent of the compensation sought. There is no 'discovery' procedure, whereby relevant documents are disclosed to the other side. If the claimant is successful in court, the damages awards are low. Most legal disputes are settled without the need for a court hearing or they are decided using private arbitrators or conciliations as a form of alternative dispute resolution.

JAPANESE COMPANY LAW

Japan's company law is based on the **Corporations Code 2006**. The basic types of Japanese companies are:

❖ Kabushiki kaisha (K.K.), similar to a UK public company;
❖ Godo kaisha (GDK), similar to a UK limited company;
❖ Goshi kaisha (GSK), similar to a UK limited liability partnership;
❖ Gomei kaisha (GMK), similar to a UK partnership.

Directors' duties and shareholder liability rules are similar to the UK system in many respects.

PEOPLE'S REPUBLIC OF CHINA

China is the great economic success story of the past quarter-century. China has opened up to the world and there are now more business and sales opportunities for UK businesses. Indeed, between 1999 and 2009 there has been a staggering 436 per cent increase in the value of UK exports to China. However, although this is good news, it also means that UK businesses are exposed to greater legal risks. As China's economy continues to expand and develop, the demand for energy resources, infrastructure, technology and goods and services is growing exponentially. Obtaining an understanding of Chinese business culture and the importance placed on good relationships is vital.

Following the Communist Party's victory in 1949, the People's Republic of China (PRC) became the world's largest communist country and created a system of socialist law derived from the former Soviet Union. With the Sino-Soviet split and the Chinese Cultural Revolution, all legal work was suspected of being counter-revolutionary and the legal system collapsed.

A need to reconstruct a legal system to prevent abuses of official authority was needed and in 1982 the National People's Congress adopted a new state constitution that emphasised rule of law to which all would be accountable. More than 300 laws and regulations – mostly economic – have been promulgated.

In drafting the new laws, the PRC has declined to copy any other legal system and the general pattern has been to issue laws for a specific topic or location. Often, laws are drafted on a trial basis, with the law being redrafted after several years. This process of creating a legal infrastructure piecemeal has led to many situations where the laws are missing, confusing or contradictory, and has caused judicial decisions having more precedent value than in most other civil law countries. In formulating laws, the PRC has been influenced by a number of sources, including traditional Chinese views towards the role of law, the PRC's socialist background, the German-based law of the Republic of China on Taiwan and the English-based common law used in Hong Kong. United States banking and securities law has also been very influential. Disputes are resolved through the use of mediation committees. These are informed groups of citizens who resolve about 90 per cent of the PRC's civil disputes and some minor criminal cases at no cost to the parties. There are more than 800,000 such committees in both rural and urban areas.

The 1982 State Constitution established four levels of courts. Judges are elected to serve a maximum of two five-year terms. A bench of one to three judges and three to five assessors will hear a case at trial. Assessors are elected by local residents or people's congresses or may be appointed by the court for their expertise. Trials are carried out in an inquisitorial manner in which both judges and assessors play an active role in questioning all witnesses. After the judge(s) and assessors have ruled on a case before them, they pass sentence. An aggrieved claimant can appeal to a higher court. The court system also requires adjudication committees to be established for courts at every level. These committees are usually made up of the president, vice-presidents, chief judges and associate chief judges of the court, who are appointed and removed by the standing committees of the people's congresses at the corresponding level. The adjudication committees are responsible for reviewing major cases to find errors of fact or law and to determine if a chief judge should withdraw from a case. If a case is submitted to an adjudication committee, the court is bound by its decision. The Supreme People's Court in Beijing is the highest court of the judicial structure and the ultimate appellate court. It is directly responsible to the National People's Congress Standing Committee, which elects the court president.

The PRC government prioritised law reform in the 1990s in order to enhance the predictability and certainty of legal outcomes. There have been great efforts to improve the legal framework and institutions such as the legislature, judiciary and legal profession. The PRC constitution and laws provide for fundamental human rights, including due process, but some have argued that they are often ignored in practice.

In 2002, the PRC became a member of the World Trade Organization (WTO) and as a result is becoming more open to international business. However, the PRC prohibits 100 per cent foreign ownership of a business and will only entertain the presence of a foreign business if it enters into a joint venture with a Chinese entity.

THE MIDDLE EAST, ISLAMIC LAW AND THE KORAN

The world's population is approximately 20 per cent Muslim. Islam is the principal religion of Afghanistan, Algeria, Bangladesh, Egypt, Indonesia, Iran, Jordan, Kuwait, Libya, Malaysia, Mali, Mauritania, Morocco, Niger, North Yemen, Oman, Pakistan, Qatar, Saudi Arabia, Somalia, South Yemen, Sudan, Syria, Tunisia, Turkey and the United Arab Emirates.

Islamic law or *Sharia* is the only law in Saudi Arabia. In other Islamic countries, the *Sharia* forms the basis of family law but coexists with other laws. The Islamic legal system is based on the teaching of the Koran, the Sunna (decisions and sayings of the prophet Muhammad) and reasoning by Islamic scholars. By the tenth century AD, Islamic scholars had decided that no further amendment or improvement of the divine law was possible, resulting in Islamic law remaining static. Islamic law was literally frozen in time.

In terms of business law, Islamic law prohibits *riba*, or the making of unearned or unjustified profit. However, making a profit from the sale of goods or the provision of services is allowed. In terms of loans and banking, the prohibition of *riba* means that the payment of interest on loans is prohibited. There are two lawful ways to get around the prohibition against *riba*. The party with money is permitted to buy an item and sell it to the other party at a profit or to advance the money and become a trading partner who shares in the profits of the enterprise. The modern reality is that Islamic law is mostly used for marriage, divorce, inheritance and criminal law. In practice, the *Sharia* is often downplayed in commercial transactions.

HINDU LAW – *DHARMASASTRA*

Hindus make up approximately 20 per cent of the world's population. Hindus are mostly found in India, where they form 80 per cent of the population, and others live in Burma, Kenya, Malaysia, Pakistan, Singapore, Tanzania and Uganda. Hindu law is derived from the ancient Hindu religion. Accordingly, Hindus respect this religious law, regardless of their nationality or place of residence. Classical Hindu law is based on the works of private scholars, which were passed on orally for many centuries before being recorded in the *smitris* (law books). Hindu law, called *dharmasastra* in Sanskrit, is the doctrine of 'proper behaviour' and is linked to the divine revelation of Veda (the holy collection of Indian religious songs, prayers, hymns and sayings, written between 2000 and 1000 BC). The subject matter of the law relates mainly to family law and succession. Anglo-Hindu law began to develop when India became a British colony in 1772. However, when the country gained independence in 1947, the Anglo-Hindu law declined. In the 1950s, India codified Hindu law by enacting a raft of legislation, including the **Constitution of India 1950**, the **Hindu Marriage Act 1955**, the **Hindu Minority and Guardianship Act 1956**, the **Hindu Succession Act 1956** and the **Hindu Adoptions and Maintenance Act 1956**.

QUESTION 21

A new oilfield is discovered in western China. Two large oil companies – Shellvron UK plc and State China Oil – would each like to drill for oil there, but neither has the resources to do so alone. Shellvron has the technical expertise to assist State China Oil to exploit the new oilfield and State China Oil has local knowledge and was established with the authority of the National People's Congress Standing Committee. Each party has £50 million to invest in the project. How could the parties pursue this project?

Answer Plan

This is a practical problem question that requires the student to demonstrate knowledge of the Anglo-American legal concept of the joint venture (JV) arrangement, as well as the legal system of the People's Republic of China (PRC).

❖   Explain the structure of a JV and a JV corporation.
❖   Illustrate with a real-life example.
❖   Consider which country will have jurisdiction over the JV and what will happen if there are disputes between the joint venturers.

ANSWER

The People's Republic of China (PRC) categorises foreign investment projects into four categories:

1.   encouraged;
2.   permitted;
3.   restricted;
4.   prohibited.

Usually, the PRC will only entertain the presence of a foreign business, such as Shellvron UK plc, operating within China if it enters into a Sino-foreign equity JV with an approved Chinese entity. Joint ventures in the energy sector are encouraged, especially those involving the extraction techniques of oil and natural gas. In addition, projects that use human and material resources in the western region of China and which are in keeping with China's industrial policies will be given preferential treatment.

A JV is an arrangement in which two or more business entities combine their resources to pursue a single project, such as to exploit a newly discovered oilfield. A JV resembles a partnership, except that partnerships are usually formed to pursue ongoing business operations rather than to focus on a single project or transaction.

It is recommended that the parties agree to join together to form a 50:50 JV partnership and that they each contribute their £50 million capital to the venture. This was the form of arrangement used by the international coffee business Starbucks when it expanded its operations into China by entering into a 50:50 JV with Shanghai President Coffee Corporation, a Chinese company. Unless otherwise agreed, joint venturers have equal rights to manage the JV. Joint venturers owe each other fiduciary duties of loyalty and care. If a joint venturer violates these duties, it is liable for the damages that flow from the breach.

In pursuing a JV, joint venturers often form an operating company to manage the JV. This is called a JV corporation. The joint venturers are shareholders of the JV corporation and the JV corporation is liable for its own debts and obligations. The joint venturers are only liable for the debts and obligations of the JV corporation up to their capital contributions to the JV corporation.

The Chinese Government permits JV and strategic alliances (an arrangement between two or more companies in the same industry in which they agree to ally themselves to accomplish a designated objective, reducing the risk for both parties). Based on the communist government's rules in China and a culture that favours business connections, UK and other foreign companies will continue to enter the Chinese market through JVs and strategic alliances with Chinese firms. These arrangements bring together the expertise of the parties.

However, the legal documents that create the JV will usually require Chinese law to apply to the JV. In the event of a legal dispute, Shellvron UK plc will need to seek a remedy through the Chinese courts, culminating in the Supreme Court in Beijing. The central Chinese Government is desirous of ensuring its laws protect local as well as international companies and its judicial system is beginning to deliver judgments relating to commercial JVs and contractual matters.

Common Pitfalls ✗

This is an advanced business law question concerning a specialised form of business law structure. Only tackle this question if you are sufficiently proficient with legal business structures.

Aim Higher ★

Discuss the law of the venture, which is a crucial commercial decision for the parties. If the law of the venture is Chinese law, this will place a heavier burden on the UK firm should it wish to enforce its legal rights at a future date. The UK joint venture partner should be clear on the significance of the law of the venture.

QUESTION 22

Foreign business entities have generally avoided civil litigation in the People's Republic of China (PRC) in relation to commercial and corporate matters. Why is this the case and how can a foreign litigant navigate the Chinese court and legal system?

Answer Plan

This question requires the student to demonstrate basic knowledge of the Chinese legal system.

❖ Introduce the Chinese legal system and the hierarchy of the courts.
❖ Discuss Chinese civil procedure law and the availability of appeals to a higher court.
❖ Analyse the issue of 'binding precedent' in connection with the PRC National Supreme People's Court.
❖ Consider the issues of contempt of court, rules of evidence, juries, damages and awards.

ANSWER

Foreign businesses have generally avoided civil litigation in the PRC, in relation to commercial and corporate matters, due to:

❖ conservative policies towards the calculation of damages;

❖ lack of provisions in Chinese law for the recovery of legal costs; and

❖ lack of access to remedies such as a preliminary injunction.

More recently, however, the Chinese courts are beginning to deliver judgments that are encouraging foreign companies doing business in China to litigate. The PRC central government has launched several campaigns to enhance the protection of local as well as international companies. However, the art of successfully enforcing legal rights in China still relies on understanding how to litigate in China. It is important to employ appropriate tactics and strategy.

The first consideration when initiating court proceedings against a Chinese defendant is to choose a suitable jurisdiction. This relies on two factors: territory and level of court.

China has a pyramid court system with four levels of courts. The Beijing-based PRC National Supreme People's Court is at the apex, followed by the Higher People's Courts in each province and the cities under direct central government control, the Intermediate People's Courts in every major city and the Local People's Courts in various counties.

The Intermediate People's Court is the usual level of trial court for commercial matters. However, if the amount of damages claimed exceeds RMB 10 million (approx £1 million) the Higher People's Court may have jurisdiction over the dispute at first instance. An appeal will lie with the PRC National Supreme People's Court in Beijing.

The **Chinese Civil Procedure Law** allows only one appeal to a higher level of court (**ss 10** and **158**). A party may apply to rehear the case if it is not happy with the judgment on appeal within two years after the judgment becomes effective. During the application period, the effectiveness of the judgment is not affected: **s 178**.

Chinese courts do not have an Anglo-American common-law system of following judicial precedent. The judges stress that they decide issues on a case-by-case basis, although they may refer to decisions in other provinces for guidance. Even if judges wanted to follow precedent, there is no equivalent to the continuous published decisions available in the Commonwealth or the United States. Companies have tried to publish various types of Chinese case reports, but this has not been commercially successful.

The one recognised binding precedent is from the PRC National Supreme People's Court. Chinese lawyers say it 'becomes the law' as befitting a code approach. For some decisions, the court issues interpretations. However, even they are not universally applicable. Similarly, China has no set of codified regulations. Parties seeking to enforce commercial rights are advised to enquire of local officials about unpublished regulations or customs.

A Chinese civil law case has the familiar steps of:

❖ determining jurisdiction;
❖ complaint;
❖ court investigation;
❖ hearing; and
❖ decision.

At the hearing the parties can present expert witnesses. On the whole, procedures are more formal and impose a higher standard of proof than the English notion of 'on the balance of probabilities'. Chinese Rules of Evidence are not terribly comprehensive in comparison with those of most Anglo-American countries. Chinese courts follow their own Rules of Civil Procedure. These do not include the equivalent of pre-trial discovery under which the parties must exchange evidence. The format for dealing with cases is more European than Anglo-American. Judges are quite active in questioning in line with the European civil law 'inquisitorial' procedure.

One particularly important omission from the Chinese court's power is that it has no power of civil contempt to force attendance at trial. From a Western perspective, this would seem to make enforcement virtually impossible. This also hinders local Chinese interests as the Chinese court's lack of power to compel attendance is detrimental to Chinese claimants seeking to enforce rights against a foreign entity.

China has no jury system. Some courts may include a technical expert as a voting member on the panel of judges. The relevant national, provincial or local ruling body selects chief judges. The chief judge then chooses the rest of the judges. The judiciary and the justice system are afforded a considerably lower professional, social and political status and respect than is the case in the West.

In the end, the judiciary can impose civil damages and penalties. However, another practical problem with damages recovery is that most Chinese corporations are not publicly traded corporations and do not have financial disclosure requirements. The level of enforcement of the judgment varies from province to province, so it is important to know local officials. The levels of enforcement provided by Beijing and Shanghai courts and those located along the southern coast are generally fairly adept. Costs of bringing a legal action are relatively modest, in the area of RMB 100 to RMB 30,000 plus legal costs.

Common Pitfalls ✘

This is an advanced question which requires the student to have a sound knowledge of both the English legal system and the Chinese legal system.

Aim Higher ★

Critically analyse the effectiveness of the Chinese legal system and how procedural matters distinguish it from the English legal system.

QUESTION 23

In February 2008, the Archbishop of Canterbury stated that the adoption of certain aspects of *Sharia* law in the UK 'seems unavoidable'. Muslim *Sharia* courts are allegedly now lawfully operating in the UK. The Muslim Arbitration Tribunal allegedly runs the courts as a result of taking advantage of a clause in the **Arbitration Act 1996**. What would be the implications of *Sharia* tribunals coexisting with English common-law courts?

Answer Plan

This is a topical essay question facing the current generation of students. It invites the student to think about the implications of introducing a religion-based legal system to coexist alongside the English legal system and any potential conflicts between the two systems that may arise.

- ❖ Introduce and explain the nature of *Sharia* law.
- ❖ Discuss the classification of *Sharia* arbitration tribunals under the **Arbitration Act 1996** to deal with civil matters.
- ❖ Illustrate the issue by discussing the long-standing existence of Jewish Beth Din Arbitration Tribunals in Britain.
- ❖ Discuss the concerns with the existence of 'parallel legal systems' within Britain.

ANSWER

Islamic *Sharia* law, which derives from the teachings of the Koran and from the Sunna (the practice of the prophet Muhammad), is implemented to varying degrees in different Islamic countries – from the beheadings of Saudi Arabia to the relatively liberal social mores of Malaysia.

Islamic law has been officially adopted in Britain, with *Sharia* courts given powers to rule on Muslim civil cases. Previously, the rulings of *Sharia* courts in Britain could not be enforced and depended on voluntary compliance among Muslims. However, the British government has effectively sanctioned the powers of *Sharia* judges to rule on civil cases ranging from divorce and financial disputes to those involving domestic violence. *Sharia* courts with these powers have been set up in London, Birmingham, Bradford and Manchester with the network's headquarters in Nuneaton, Warwickshire. *Sharia* currently has no jurisdiction in Scotland, nor is there any intention to introduce it. Rulings issued by a network of five *Sharia* courts are enforceable with the full power of the judicial system, through the county courts or High Court.

The Muslim Arbitration Tribunal runs the courts, taking advantage of a clause in the **Arbitration Act 1996**. Under the Act, the *Sharia* courts are classified as arbitration tribunals. The Act allows disputes to be resolved using alternative methods of dispute resolution such as tribunals. The rulings of arbitration tribunals are binding in law, provided that both parties in the dispute agree to give it the power to rule on their case.

The disclosure that Muslim courts have legal powers in Britain occurred several months after the Archbishop of Canterbury's comment that the establishment of certain aspects of *Sharia* law 'seems unavoidable' in Britain.

Lord Chief Justice Phillips, the head of the judiciary, also confirmed that *Sharia* law could be used to settle marital and financial disputes. In fact, Muslim *Sharia* tribunals started passing *Sharia* judgments in August 2007. They have dealt with cases ranging from Muslim divorce and inheritance to nuisance neighbours. It was also reported that the tribunals have settled cases of domestic violence between married couples, working together with the police investigations.

It is interesting to note that Jewish Beth Din tribunals also operate under the same provision in the **Arbitration Act** to resolve civil cases, according to Jewish religious law. Jewish Beth Din religious tribunals have existed in Britain for over a century, and previously operated under an earlier version of the **Arbitration Act**.

There are concerns that the development of Muslim *Sharia* tribunals could be the start of a 'parallel legal system', based on Islamic *Sharia* law, for some British Muslims. An example of where *Sharia* and British law conflict relates to the law of inheritance, because Islamic law favours male heirs. It was reported that in an inheritance dispute handled by the *Sharia* Tribunal in Nuneaton, the estate of a Midlands Muslim man was divided between three daughters and two sons. The *Sharia* judges on the panel awarded the sons a share of the estate that was twice as large as that of the daughters, in accordance with *Sharia*. In a British court, the estate would have been divided equally between the siblings.

In June 2011, Baroness Cox, an independent peer, introduced a Private Member's Bill entitled the **Arbitration and Mediation Services (Equality) Bill** to ensure *Sharia* tribunals and councils operate within the law and do not form a concurrent legal system within the UK. Baroness Cox is particularly concerned that women are being discriminated against within *Sharia* courts and that they are being deprived of their legal rights.

Traditionally, the English legal system has supported the principle that there is only one law for everybody and that this is an important pillar of our social identity as a Western democracy. The concern from the non-Islamic British community is in allowing *Sharia* civil law tribunals, which would eventually lead to the use of the harsher Islamic laws (as in parts of the Middle East, including Iran and Saudi Arabia) for Hadd criminal offences. Punishment can include stoning, lashes or amputation of a hand. Sexual offences carry a penalty of stoning to death or flogging, while theft is punished by amputation. These types of punishment would not be tolerated in Britain. There are also concerns about the standard of proof applied in *Sharia* tribunals. However, if Jewish tribunals are allowed to continue to operate a 'parallel civil law legal system', it is difficult to see how it is possible to deny the existence of Islamic *Sharia* civil law tribunals, especially in 'predominantly Muslim' areas of Britain.

Common Pitfalls ✘

Essentially you are being asked to describe a foreign law system. Where possible, draw explicit comparisons with the English legal system.

Aim Higher ★

Aim to explain the relevance of the foreign laws for the contemporary, domestic English law issues. Evaluate the significant ways in which the foreign law differs from domestic law or the reasons why those involved in the English law system ought to be interested in it. Consider whether there is any functional equivalent or not.

Contract Law and E-commerce

INTRODUCTION

A contract is an agreement enforceable at law and is the basis of the business world's commercial activities. Contracts provide the means for people and businesses to sell property, services and other rights. Selling a car or computers is based on a sales contract; engaging an employee is based on a contract of service; the lease of premises is based on a rental contract; over the internet, the sale of goods and services is based on electronic contracts. Without enforceable contracts, commerce would break down. The parties enter into contracts voluntarily and are free to agree on the terms they wish, subject to legislation enacted to protect consumers, debtors and others from unfair contracts. The courts must enforce the terms of the contract if a party fails to perform the contract. The source of contract law is the common law of contracts, which developed from early court decisions that became precedent for later decisions.

An essential feature of contract is a promise by one party to another to do or forbear from doing certain specified acts. The offer of a promise becomes a promise by acceptance. A contract is that species of agreement whereby a legal obligation is created and defined between two or more parties.

For a contract to be valid and legally enforceable there must be:

❖ offer and acceptance;
❖ intention to create legal relations;
❖ consideration given by both parties;
❖ legal capacity to contract; and
❖ no vitiating factors such as duress or illegal subject matter.

Once a valid contract has been agreed, the parties must honour the terms of the contract or face the legal consequence of breaking or breaching the contract. If a party breaches a contract, legal remedies will be available to the other party, which can enforce their contractual claim in court.

The cyberspace economy is now upon us as the use of computer technology and the internet has spread. A new form of commerce – electronic commerce or e-commerce – is a relatively new development to the common law of contracts.

E-commerce has created difficulties in relation to:

1.   The issue of when a contract is formed over the internet;
2.   The enforcement of e-contracts; and
3.   The provision of consumer protection.

Even to date, there has been little case law decided by the courts on the subject of contracts created over the internet.

QUESTION 24

How can one distinguish between an offer and an invitation to treat? Support and illustrate your answer with references to relevant case law.

Answer Plan

❖   Explain the nature of an 'offer' in the context of contract law.
❖   Compare an 'offer' with an 'invitation to treat'. Explain how they differ.
❖   Illustrate an 'invitation to treat' with reference to *Partridge v Crittenden* (1968).
❖   Consider requests for tender as invitation to treat.
❖   Consider the issue of websites offering goods and services for sale.

ANSWER

It is important to be able to distinguish between an offer and an invitation to treat as each has very different legal consequences. A person who is not prepared to take on the legal consequence of the offer being accepted should not make an offer. For example, X should not agree to sell her pedigree puppy Spot to Y for £300 unless she is fully prepared to hand over the puppy, as she will be legally bound to do so. If the offer is accepted and X does not hand over the puppy on receipt of the £300, she must suffer the consequence and may be ordered by a court to hand over the dog (perform the contract) or pay damages (compensation in the amount of £300 plus legal costs and any other damages flowing from the contract).

An invitation to treat, on the other hand, is not an offer; it is only an invitation for the other party to make an offer. By way of example, an advertisement is usually only an invitation to treat, that is, to open negotiations with a view to forming a contract. There are many occasions where 'invitations to treat' are misconstrued as offers. For example, if a shop displays goods for sale with a price label attached, they are not obliged to sell for the marked price. This is because displaying goods for sale is regarded in law as merely an invitation to treat, not an offer: *Fisher v Bell* (1961); *Partridge v Crittenden* (1968). A typical contract is actually made and concluded at the checkout.

In the *Partridge v Crittenden* (1968) case, the defendant had advertised bramblefinches in a magazine at £1.25 each. A customer sent £1.25 to the defendant, who on receipt of the money sent a bramblefinch to the customer. Later, the defendant was charged with offering a live wild bird for sale, which was a breach of the **Protection of Birds Act 1964**. It was held that the defendant was not guilty by reason that his advertisement was an invitation to treat, not an offer. Consequently, the advertisement was not an 'offer for sale' of a wild bird. In fact the defendant was guilty of 'selling a wild bird', a different crime under the Act, but he had not been charged with this crime.

Requests to tender are often construed as an invitation to treat, but it will depend on the language used in the request to tender. If the advertisement asks for tenders to supply electrical cable, without stating that the lowest tender will be accepted, then the advertisement will only be an invitation to treat.

Finally, websites that advertise goods and services and the prices at which they are available will amount to invitations to treat and not offers. The buyer will accept the offer by clicking on the button. Acceptance is effective once the customer has received confirmation that his or her offer/order has been accepted.

Common Pitfalls ✗

This questions involves an evaluation of a fairly basic aspect of contract law. If you choose such a question in an exam situation, ensure you define and explain the legal terminology (offer and invitation to treat) and underpin your essay by referring to the relevant case law.

Aim Higher ★

In this essay-style question it is important to discuss the facts and principles of each relevant case in some depth to show that you have a high level of understanding of the law.

QUESTION 25

Mark sees a diamond engagement ring marked £100 in the window of Sparkles Jewellery store. He enters the shop and says to the sales assistant, 'I would like to buy the diamond ring in the window marked £100.' The sales assistant exclaims, 'I am terribly sorry, the price label should have read £1,000, so I am unable to sell you the diamond ring for £100.'

▶ Explain whether Mark has any legal rights.

Answer Plan

This is a problem question requiring the student to apply his or her legal knowledge to a set of facts and provide advice.

❖ Explain the requirement of offer and acceptance for a valid contract to exist (as one of the essential requirements).

❖ Explain the difference between an offer and an invitation to treat and apply this to the facts.

❖ Illustrate the difference by reference to authority including: *Partridge v Crittenden* (1968), *Fisher v Bell* (1960) and *Pharmaceutical Society of Great Britain v Boots Cash Chemists* (1953).

ANSWER

For a valid contract to exist, usually one party must have made an offer and the other must have accepted it. Once acceptance takes effect, a contract will usually be binding on both parties.

The person making an offer is called the offeror and the person to whom the offer is made is called the offeree. A communication will be treated as an offer if it indicates the terms on which the offeror is prepared to make a contract (such as the price of the goods for sale) and gives a clear indication that the offeror intends to be bound by those terms if they are accepted by the offeree. Here, it might seem from the facts that Mark is the offeror, but in law, is that actually the case?

Some kinds of transaction involve a preliminary stage in which one party invites the other to make an offer. This stage is called an invitation to treat. In the context of the law relating to offer and acceptance, 'invitation to treat' means to negotiate. The main significance of an invitation to treat is that it is not an offer. In the case of *Partridge v Crittenden* (1968), it was established that an advertisement that described goods and the price for which they could be purchased was an invitation to treat and as such could not form a binding contract.

Confusion can sometimes arise when what would appear, in the everyday sense of the word, to be an offer is held by the law to be only an invitation to treat. This issue arises particularly in relation to price-marked goods on display on the shelves or in the windows of shops, such as the diamond engagement ring displayed in the Sparkles Jewellery store window marked £100. In law, such a display is regarded merely as an invitation to treat, rather than an offer to sell the goods at that price.

In *Fisher v Bell* (1960), the defendant had displayed flick knives in his shop window, and was convicted of offering the knives for sale. On appeal, Lord Parker CJ stated that the display of an article with a price on it in a shop window was only an invitation to treat and not an offer, and the conviction was overturned.

There are two main practical consequences of this principle. First, shops do not have to sell goods at the marked price – so if a shop assistant wrongly marks a ring £100 rather than £1,000, Mark cannot insist on buying the ring for £100. Second, a customer cannot insist on buying a particular item on display in the window – one cannot make the shop sell you the ring in the window, even if there are none left inside the shop. Displaying the goods is not an offer, so a customer cannot accept it and thereby make a binding contract.

In *Pharmaceutical Society of Great Britain v Boots Cash Chemists* (1953) it was held that display of goods on shelves amounts to an invitation to treat. The customer's action in taking the goods from the shelves and placing them in their basket constituted an offer to buy. The customer's offer to buy was accepted when the cashier took the purchase price.

As no offer has been made it is not possible for Mark to accept and therefore no contract in law exists regarding the purchase of a ring for £100.

Common Pitfalls ✗

Read each sentence of the fact scenario carefully. Discuss the issues in the order they arise in the facts. You need to be precise in your analysis of the facts and application of the relevant provisions of the relevant case law.

Aim Higher ★

Ensure you consider the point of view of the client you are advising, in this case Mark. What outcome does he want? Identify the corresponding legal issues. In other words, what sort of legal argument needs to be advanced in order for the client to get what they want? Work your way through the various contract law issues as they arise in the question, interchangeably stating the given legal requirement or legal principle and how this might apply to the facts. Conclude by stating the possible outcome(s), in other words whether a contract exists.

QUESTION 26

Critically examine the nature of a contract entered into over the internet and in particular the requirement of offer and acceptance.

Answer plan

- ❖ Confirm the lack of relevant case law on the subject of contracts made over the internet.
- ❖ State the two most common ways for forming a contract over the internet and consider each in turn.
- ❖ Discuss the House of Lords decision in *Brinkibon Ltd v Stahag Stahl und Stahlwarenhandelsgesellschaft GmbH* (1983) and in particular, Lord Wilberforce's judgment, which, although concerning a telex communication, is relevant to contracts made over the internet.
- ❖ Consider the effects of the **Electronic Commerce (EC Directive) Regulations 2002** and the **Consumer Protection (Distance Selling) Regulations 2000**.

ANSWER

To date there have been no important UK court decisions concerning when a contract is concluded over the internet. The two key means for making a contract over the internet are as follows:

(1) By exchange of emails; or
(2) Buying goods or services by visiting a website and paying online.

In relation to the first method, where emails have been exchanged, the rule relating to letters – the postal rule – which originated in the case of *Adams v Lindsell*

(1818), should apply. The court will objectively consider the contents of the email to determine whether it should be construed as an invitation to treat, an offer or an acceptance. What is problematic is deciding the exact moment when an acceptance by email is effective. The difficulty is that the person sending the email does not know precisely when the email is received unless a 'receipt return' is included when the message is sent. In the House of Lords decision in *Brinkibon Ltd v Stahag Stahl und Stahlwarenhandelsgesellschaft GmbH* (1983), on the subject of a communication by telex, Lord Wilberforce confirmed that the court will take a common-sense, yet adaptable approach. He stated:

> The message may not reach, or be intended to reach, the designated recipient immediately: Messages may be sent out of office hours, or at night, with the intention, or on the assumption, that they will be read at a later time. There may be some error or default at the recipient's end which prevents receipt at the time contemplated and believed in by the sender ... And many other variations may occur. No universal rule can cover all such cases; they must be resolved by reference to the intentions of the parties, by sound business practice and in some cases by a judgment where the risks should lie.

Basically, Lord Wilberforce is saying that the courts will adopt a flexible approach and consider the intentions of the parties, practical business sense and where the risk should lie in a given situation. In essence, the court confirms that it will objectively consider the contents of the email(s) to determine whether the communications between the parties should be construed as an invitation to treat, an offer or an acceptance.

In conclusion, the EU has legislated on the matter of which formalities must be complied with when a contract is made with an internet service provider (ISP) in the **Electronic Commerce (EC Directive) Regulations 2002**. However, these Regulations do not cover the time at which the contract is concluded. Regardless, consumers have the right to cancel concluded distance contracts (including contracts made over the internet) via the **Consumer Protection (Distance Selling) Regulations 2000**.

Common Pitfalls ✗

This is an essay question that could potentially be answered in a wide range of ways, but you are specifically directed to discuss the issues of offer and acceptance. Ensure you narrow your discussion and deal with each of these topics. Students should also be wary of writing an answer with 'too much opinion, and not enough law'.

Aim Higher ★

Credit will be given for critically examining in depth why the traditional contract law analysis of a transaction entered into over the internet is problematic. This is a case where society is comfortable with the concept of entering into legally binding contracts, but the law has struggled to adapt and deal with new technology.

QUESTION 27

Distinguish between the following contract law terms:

(1) Bilateral and unilateral contracts;
(2) Express and implied contracts;
(3) Executory and executed and past consideration;
(4) Sufficient consideration and adequate consideration;
(5) Void and voidable contracts.

Answer Plan

This is a subdivided question. Answer (1) to (5) in turn, clearly identifying each section by number and in order. Unless you are told otherwise, it is reasonable for you to assume that each section carries equal marks. This means that each section is worth 20 per cent and you should allocate equal time to each subsection. The purpose of this question is to assess the student's general knowledge across the topic of contract law.

ANSWER

(1) Contracts are either bilateral or unilateral, depending on what the offeree must do to accept the offeror's offer. A bilateral contract is entered into by way of an exchange of promises between the parties. In other words, a promise for a promise. The offer of a promise becomes a promise by acceptance. Most contracts are bilateral (two-sided) because each party makes a promise to the other. For example, the seller has agreed to sell the product and the buyer has agreed to pay the price. A unilateral contract, on the other hand, is one in which the offeror's offer is only by the performance of an act by the offeree; in other words, a promise for an act. No contract exists until the offeree performs the requested act.

(2) A contract may be express or implied. Express contracts are stated orally or in writing by the parties. An agreement between one business to buy office furniture from another business is an example of a written contract. An agreement by a person to sell his bicycle to his neighbour is an oral contract. However, contracts can also be implied from the conduct of the parties. The following elements must be established to create a contract implied by conduct:

i. one party provided property or services to the other party;
ii. the party expected to be paid by the other party for the property or services and did not provide the services for free;
iii. the receiving party was given an opportunity to reject the property or services but did not do so.

(3) A valuable consideration in the sense of the law may consist either in some right, interest, profit or benefit accruing to one party, or some forbearance, detriment, loss or responsibility given, suffered or undertaken by the other: *Curie v Misa* (1875) *per* Lush J. An executed consideration is some value given in a way which has completely fulfilled a party's liability under the contract. In the *Carlill v Carbolic Smoke Ball Company* (1893) case, Mrs Carlill simply used the smoke ball. The only contractual liability remains with the other party; in this case the Smoke Ball Company still had to pay Mrs Carlill the reward (executory consideration). Conversely, a promise to do some act which has previously been done is no consideration because it is a promise to do nothing. It is a common-law principle that 'past consideration is no consideration'. However, if two conditions are satisfied, a past act can be good consideration. First, the other party must have asked for the act to be done. Second, both parties must always have contemplated that payment would be made.

(4) It is a common-law principle of contract law that 'consideration must be sufficient but need not be adequate'. This statement of law is mystifying because in plain English the words 'sufficient' and 'adequate' mean virtually the same thing. However, in contract law, if consideration is 'sufficient' it means that the consideration in question must be of some recognisable value, even if very minor. If the consideration does not need to be adequate, it means that the consideration does not have to be of equal value for each party. A practical example is regarding the purchase of a computer. If the purchaser pays the shop the usual sale price of £400, then both his and the shop's consideration is sufficient because it has some value, and adequate because the promise to pay is worth about the same as the promise to give ownership of the computer. If the purchaser only paid £1 for the computer the consideration would have been sufficient because £1 has value, however small, but not adequate because the computer is probably in fact worth more than £1, so the consideration provided by the purchase and the shop are not equal. The law does not concern itself with adequacy because it is difficult to put a price on an item of property, and further,

if a party makes a bad (unequal) contract s/he should not be able to avoid the contract.

(5) When a contract is void, no contract exists. A void contract has no legal effect. It is as if no contract had ever been created. For example, a contract to commit a crime is void. If a contract is void, neither party is obligated to perform the terms of the contract and neither party can enforce the contract against the other. Whereas, when a contract is voidable, a party has the option to avoid the contract and his contractual obligations. If the contract is avoided, both parties are released from their obligations under the contract. If the party with the option chooses to ratify the contract, both parties must fully perform their contractual obligations. With certain exceptions, contract may be avoided by minors, mentally incapable persons, intoxicated persons or persons acting under duress or undue influence or fraud, and in cases involving mutual mistake.

Common Pitfalls ✗

The question requires you to legally analyse the contract law terms listed as (1) to (5). In terms of structure of the answer it is important to briefly introduce the topic of contract law generally. It would, however, be a mistake not to mirror the (1) to (5) structure in writing your answer. This question comprises five parts, each involving issues of similar complexity, so make sure your answer is appropriately balanced between these parts.

Aim Higher ★

Where possible, when explaining and distinguishing the relevant contract law terms, illustrate the terms by referring to relevant case law.

QUESTION 28

Consider the extent to which the **Contracts (Rights of Third Parties) Act 1999** has changed the law relating to privity of contract.

Answer Plan

❖ Define the phrase 'privity of contract'; illustrate with relevant pre-1999 case law such as *Tweddle v Atkinson* (1861) and *Dunlop Pneumatic Tyre Co Ltd v Selfridge & Co Ltd* (1915).

❖ Illustrate the problem sometimes caused by the privity rule by referring to *Daniels and Daniels v R White & Sons Ltd and Tarbard* (1938) and *Jackson v Horizon Holidays Ltd* (1975).

❖ Discuss the aim of the **Contract (Rights of Third Parties) Act 1999**.

❖ Consider the impact of the legislation on the common law.

ANSWER

Privity of contract is the relationship that exists between the immediate parties to a contract, which is necessary to enable one person to sue another on it. In essence, a contract is private between the parties who agreed it. Anyone who did not enter into the contract cannot sue on the contract or, indeed, be sued on the contract.

There is now legislation that governs the issue of privity of contract that has applied since 1999, but it is interesting to examine the pre-1999 case law to help illustrate the point. The privity rule was established in the case of *Tweddle v Atkinson* (1861). In this case William Guy and John Tweddle entered into a contract with each other. It was a term of the contract that Guy would pay Tweddle's son (who was to marry Guy's daughter) the sum of £200. In return, John Tweddle would pay Guy £100. The contract provided that Tweddle's son would be entitled to sue either his father John or his intended bride's father Guy. John Tweddle paid as promised, but Guy died before he could carry out his part of the bargain. Tweddle's son sued Guy's personal representative seeking payment from the estate. As personal representatives, they had taken over the obligation. However, the court held that Tweddle's son could not sue on the contract because he did not make the contract and therefore did not have standing to sue. The privity rule was affirmed in later case law such as *Dunlop Pneumatic Tyre Co Ltd v Selfridge & Co Ltd* (1915) House of Lords.

The problem with the privity rule, which led to the new legislation, was that in some cases it could cause injustice when one person bought unsafe goods or services on behalf of another, as happened in the cases of *Daniels and Daniels v R White & Sons Ltd and Tarbard* (1938) and *Jackson v Horizon Holidays Ltd* (1975).

The legislation – the **Contracts (Rights of Third Parties) Act 1999** – altered but did not abolish the privity rule. This Act now provides for two ways in which a third party can sue on a contract; if the contract:

(1) expressly states that the third party is entitled to have the right to sue on the contract (**s 1(1)(a)** of the Act);

(2) intended to confer a benefit on the third party then the third party is entitled to sue on the contract to enforce this benefit (**s 1(1)(b)** of the Act).

In relation to (1) above, for example, a woman might buy a washing machine for her daughter and the contract might say that if the washing machine is not of satisfactory quality, the daughter could sue the seller on the contract. If this reasoning was applied, then the case of *Tweddle v Atkinson* (1861) would be decided differently and the son would have been permitted to sue Guy's estate to enforce his entitlement to the £200 payment.

In order for (1) or (2) to be valid, **s 1(3)** of the Act provides that the third party's name must be included in the contract. When a benefit is conferred on a third party by the Act, the third party is entitled to any remedy that would have been available to her or him if s/he had made the contract her-/himself.

It is clear that the Act has made the privity rule less strict as now there are two exceptions to it, particularly in situations where a contract is made for the benefit of another.

Common Pitfalls ✗

In this essay question it is important to discuss BOTH the relevant case law AND the impact of the legislation. Failure to discuss one form of law or the other would be regarded as a serious omission.

Aim Higher ★

Additional marks will be gained for demonstrating how the law applies to the facts and showing how the Act would have changed the pre-Act cases such as *Tweddle v Atkinson* (1831).

QUESTION 29

The details of six potential contracts are set out below. Advise on the validity of each contract.

(1) Josephine Kidd, a successful Oscar-winning actress, agrees to give the Labour Party a political donation of one million pounds in return for a damehood.

Business Library - Issue Receipt

Customer name: Mphaya, Flora Samantha

Title: Business law : 2012-2013 / Janice
Denoncourt.
ID: 1006894343
Due: 20 Jan 2014 23:59

Total items: 1
25/11/2013 10:59

All items must be returned before the due date
and time.
The loan period may be shortened if the item is
requested.

(2) Miss Catherine Clever, an employee in a firm that runs a successful hedge fund in the City of London, initiates a case in the Employment Tribunal against her boss for sexual harassment and discrimination. She agrees to drop the case against him in exchange for a payment of £200,000.

(3) Lewis Jets enters into a contract to sell 30 fighter planes to the Taliban in the Islamic Republic of Afghanistan.

(4) Justine agrees to pay her friend Theunis £500 to beat up her ex-husband Marco, who has not paid his child support payment for the last six months.

(5) A prostitute hires a luxury caravan for the purpose of attracting a higher class of clientele.

(6) Johan, a software engineer, is an employee of IT Solutions Ltd. He decides to resign in order to start his own consulting firm. It is a term of his employment agreement (that he signed when he joined the company five years ago following his graduation from university) that he would not compete with IT Solutions Ltd for a period of ten years from the date of his resignation.

Answer Plan

This is a subdivided question. Answer (1) to (6) in turn, clearly identifying each section by number and in order. Unless you are told otherwise, it is reasonable for you to assume that each section carries equal marks. This means that each section is worth approximately 16.5 per cent and you should allocate equal time to each subsection. The purpose of this question is to assess the student's general knowledge across the topic of illegal and void contracts.

❖ Introduce the topic of contracts illegal at law on the basis that a contract may be illegal either at common law or because a statute makes it illegal. The illegality may relate to the nature of the contract itself, or as to the way in which it is performed.

❖ Confirm the consequences that flow from an illegal contract, namely, that if a contract is illegal then it will generally be unenforceable.

❖ Note that certain types of contracts, while not illegal, are void because they contravene public policy.

❖ Set out the types of contracts that are illegal at common law.

❖ Apply this to your analysis of the fact scenarios in (1) to (6) and reach a conclusion as to whether the contract in question is valid or void.

ANSWER

Illegal contracts are void *ab initio* at common law, provided the illegality was present at the time the contract was formed. There are many types of contract that are illegal and void *ab initio* at common law:

a. Contracts that are in restraint of trade;
b. Contracts that attempt to oust the jurisdiction of the courts;
c. Contracts that are damaging to the institution of marriage;
d. Contracts that are to commit a crime, tort or fraud;
e. Contracts threatening to damage foreign relations or the safety of the public in the UK;
f. Contracts to pervert the course of justice, such as a contract to commit perjury;
g. Contracts causing corruption in public life;
h. Contracts promoting sexual immorality.

Where a contract has been tainted by illegality and lawful provisions exist within it, the entire contract will be void *ab initio*. We will examine each of the six potential contracts in turn and analyse their validity. Turning to the potential contracts listed in (1) to (6) above, set out below is an analysis of the validity of each potential contract.

1. 'Ms Kidd's donation in return for a damehood' – This is an illegal contract because it is a contract that tends to promote corruption in public life. A case in point to support this conclusion is *Parkinson v College of Ambulance Ltd* (1925). In this case the claimant was promised that he would receive a knighthood if he made a donation to a charity. He made the donation, but did not receive the award and took legal action to enforce the contract. His action failed because the contract was illegal. The contract is void.

2. 'Miss Clever's agreement to settle her harassment and discrimination case for £200,000' – A contract such as this, namely, not to pursue a civil action is perfectly valid as it is not a contract that impedes the administration of justice. In fact, just the opposite, 'settling out of court' is exactly what happens in over 90 per cent of cases. Agreeing to accept compensation is binding on both the parties because it is a contractual promise. The consideration is Miss Clever's promise not to sue in exchange for the boss's £200,000 compensation payment. The terms of the agreement would usually be recorded in writing and submitted to the court. It is public policy that once a matter has been settled out of court it cannot be reopened.

3. 'Lewis Jets' contract to sell 30 fighter planes to the Taliban' – In times of war certain nations become enemy nations. This contract is clearly a contract to trade with an enemy of the UK and is usually held to be void. In other words, it is as if the contract never existed. Neither party could enforce the contract through a UK court.

4. 'Justine's contract to pay Theunis £500 to beat up Marco' – A contract to commit the crime of grievous bodily harm/assault is illegal and therefore void. The authority for this proposition is found in the centuries-old case *Everet v Williams* (1725), in which a highwayman tried to sue on a contract with another

highwayman to jointly rob a stagecoach. The claimant failed in this action and, indeed, both he and the defendant were hanged and the solicitors were fined £50 for bringing the case!

5. 'A prostitute hiring a luxury caravan to improve her business prospects' – This contract would likely be classified as a contract tending to promote sexual immorality, which is illegal and void. The facts are analogous to the fact in the case of *Pearce v Brooks* (1866), where a prostitute hired a carriage that the owner knew was to be used for immoral purposes. The prostitute refused to pay for the hire of the carriage, but the owner was not allowed to recover the agreed payments because it was deemed to be an illegal contract.

6. 'Johan's contract with his former employer' – The clause in Johan's employment contract restraining him from competing (setting up in the same business as his employer) for a period of ten years is against public policy because of the duration of the restraint. A court would regard the period of ten years as excessive and unreasonable: *Fitch v Dawes* (1921). A restraint of, say, six months would probably be reasonable because Johan might have knowledge of trade secrets, trade connections, client lists or other confidential information. As such, the clause is void and not enforceable by IT Solutions. This means that Johan is free to start his own consulting business. It is generally desirable that people should be able to carry on their trade, business or profession without hindrance. Therefore any contract in restraint of trade is void at common law unless it can be proved to be reasonable between the parties to the contract and reasonable as regards the public interest.

Common Pitfalls ✗

This question comprises six parts, each involving issues of similar complexity, so make sure your answer is appropriately balanced between these parts. A good paragraph on each potential contract supported by a brief statement regarding the relevant legal principle, citing the authority for same, is what is warranted in this question.

Aim Higher ★

If you get stuck on one part, skip it, leaving space in your exam paper to go back to it later. Keep moving in order to gain as many marks as possible. Timing is crucial and markers often see good answers to the first few analyses and then very flimsy answers to the remainder.

QUESTION 30

Abigail Designs is an interior decorating company. Abigail is the chief designer and has entered into a contract to decorate the foyer of the Notts Law Firm for £10,000. Five events are set out below. Discuss whether the contract has been lawfully discharged.

(1)   Both parties agree to call the contract off before Abigail Designs has started any design work.
(2)   Abigail begins work but does not want to finish the job as she wishes to immediately start work on a project for a higher paying client. Notts Law Firm does not agree to release her from the contract.
(3)   Abigail completes the first stage of the contracted design work, but is involved in a serious car accident, is hospitalised and will not be fit to return to work for a period of three months.
(4)   Abigail Designs completes the first stage of the contracted design work. In reliance on the agreed design, Notts Law Firm purchases fixtures and fittings from an independent supplier for £3,000. Shortly after, Abigail has a serious disagreement with her partner over her management of the work. Abigail walks off site and vows not to return.
(5)   Abigail Design completes the contracted design work, but Notts Law Firm only pays £7,500, instead of the £10,000 originally agreed.

Answer Plan

❖   Introduce the law surrounding the issue of discharge of contract, that is, that the contract has been completed and is no longer binding.
❖   Briefly outline the ways in which a contract may be discharged, that is, performance, agreement, breach, frustration or statutory cooling-off period.
❖   Apply the law to each of (1) to (5), referring to relevant case law to support your arguments and conclusions.

ANSWER

When a contract is made between the parties, contractual liability arises to perform the agreed terms. When the parties have both fully performed their obligations under the contract, it is discharged and ceases to exist. Contracts can be discharged by one of five ways, namely: (1) by performance; (2) by agreement; (3) by frustration; (4) by breach; or (5) by a statutory cooling-off period.

(1)   Abigail and Notts Law Firm have agreed to call off the contract before there has been any performance of it. This means that the parties have abandoned the

contract and effectively they have discharged their obligations under the contract by agreement. This has in fact created a new agreement between the parties. First, Notts Law Firm has given consideration to Abigail by discharging her from her obligation to decorate its foyer. Abigail has given Notts Law Firm consideration by discharging it from the obligation to pay her.

(2) In this case, Abigail has partially performed the contract as she has only begun to decorate Notts Law Firm's foyer. She will be in breach of the contract if she does not complete the work and fully perform the contract. Notts Law Firm refuse to accept partial performance of the contract and want the job completed. There is a general rule that where the partial performance is substantial (i.e. almost complete) then it will have to be paid for. Unfortunately, Abigail cannot rely on the substantial performance rule because she has only just begun the work and it is not substantially complete. Accordingly, Notts Law Firm can refuse to pay for the work carried out and sue for damages: *Sumpter v Hedges* (1898).

(3) Abigail has been prevented from performing her obligations under the contract due to the car accident leaving her incapacitated and unfit for work. The contract to decorate the foyer may have become frustrated if it is impossible to perform. In other words, a perfectly valid contract has become impossible to perform due to a party's incapacitation. A case in point (with similar facts) is *Condor v The Barron Knights Ltd* (1966). In this case, the claimant was a drummer who had a contract with a band to perform seven nights a week for five years and up to twice a night. One month after the contract began, the drummer collapsed and was taken to mental hospital. The band dismissed the drummer because he was unfit to work. The drummer successfully sued the band for wrongful dismissal on the grounds that his contract was frustrated as it had become impossible for him to perform in the long term. However, in Abigail's case, the decision in *Condor* could be distinguished on the basis that she should recover from the injuries sustained in the car accident within a relatively short period of three months. This would mean the contract has not been frustrated, but is merely more difficult to perform because of the delay: *Davis Contractors Ltd v Fareham UDC* (1956).

(4) Abigail has refused to continue with the contract to redecorate the Notts Law Firm's foyer due to a personal disagreement with a colleague. In effect, by refusing to abide by the terms of the contract without any legal excuse (e.g. frustration), Abigail has breached the contract. A party to the contract who has brought about a certain event cannot claim that this event frustrates the contract. The court will take the view that this event is at Abigail's risk. Self-induced frustration is no frustration. Accordingly, the contract is not at an end and Abigail will be liable to compensate Notts Law Firm if she does not fully perform her obligations under the contract.

(5) The contract between Abigail and the Notts Law Firm will not be discharged by the latter paying only £7,500, instead of £10,000. If Abigail accepts 75 per cent of

the contract price, the contract is not discharged because a lesser sum of money cannot be consideration for a greater sum owed. Abigail may waive (give up) her contractual right to the remaining £2,500 owed to her for the work by indicating to the Notts Law Firm that she will not insist on her rights. However, if Notts Law Firm does not give Abigail any consideration for her waiver, the contract is not discharged. Abigail will still have the right to seek payment for the remaining £2,500 if she chooses to exercise that right, but she must give Notts Law Firm reasonable notice of her intention. Until Abigail gives notice, Notts Law Firm cannot be in breach of the contract for failure to perform a waived right: *Charles Rickards Ltd v Oppenheim* (1950).

Common Pitfalls ✗

The question requires you to legally analyse the potential contracts listed as (1) to (5). In terms of structure of the answer it is important to briefly introduce the topic of contract law generally. It would, however, be a mistake not to mirror the (1) to (5) structure in writing your answer. This problem-style question comprises five parts, each involving issues of similar complexity, so make sure your answer is appropriately balanced between these parts.

Aim Higher ★

With a problem question, examiners are generally testing your ability to :

(a) read facts and separate narrative from real issues;

(b) identify relevant law, rather than writing everything you know about the whole subject;

(c) apply the relevant law to the facts and identify those grey areas where facts and/ or law are uncertain.

QUESTION 31

On 15 October 2010 East Midlands Airways ('EMA') advertise a second-hand Airbus 321 for sale in an aviation industry trade journal for £10.4m. Later that same day, Phil, the Chief Executive Officer of Zulu Aviation Ltd, phones EMA's Managing Director, Joseph. Phil says that his firm would very much like to view the Airbus 321 but that he is off on a five-day business trip to Zurich, Switzerland and will not be able to view the aircraft until he returns. Joseph says that if another buyer comes forward he will have to sell the Airbus 321 to that buyer. Phil then says he will pay £100,000 if EMA promises not to sell the Airbus 321 to another buyer for the next five days. Joseph agrees to this. Analyse whether any contract has been made between the parties and, if so, what are its terms? Refer to the relevant case law to support your answer.

Answer Plan

This problem question requires a careful analysis of whether a valid contract has been formed between the parties to purchase the Airbus. Follow a logical structure considering each of the legal requirements for a valid contract:

❖ By way of introduction define the legal meaning of the term 'contract'.
❖ Has a valid offer been made? Or is it merely an invitation to treat?
❖ What are the terms of the offer?
❖ Has there been acceptance of the offer (if any)?
❖ Is there intention to create legal relations?
❖ What is the consideration moving between the parties?
❖ Are there any factors that would vitiate the formation of a contract?

ANSWER

This fact situation concerns the issue of contract formation and whether a valid and legally binding agreement exists between EMA and Zulu Aviation. Agreement consists of an offer by an indication of one person (the 'offeror') to another (the 'offeree') of the offeror's willingness to enter into a contract on certain terms without further negotiations. For a contract to be valid there must be an offer, an acceptance of that offer on certain terms, an intention to create legal relations and consideration given by both parties. Once a contract has been made, both sides will be bound to honour its terms or suffer the legal consequences. The analysis that follows will examine the facts to determine whether a valid contract to purchase the Airbus exists between the parties.

DOES EMA'S ADVERTISEMENT AMOUNT TO A VALID OFFER TO CONTRACT?

Almost all contracts are made through the process of offer and acceptance. One of the parties (the offeror) makes an offer by proposing a set of terms with the intention that these terms will form a legally binding agreement if they are accepted by the party to whom they are proposed, the offeree. In this scenario, EMA initially places an advertisement. A key question is: does EMA's advertisement amount to an offer in law? It is important to make a distinction between an offer and an invitation to treat. An invitation to treat is not an offer; rather, it is an invitation to negotiate or an invitation to make an offer. In legal terms, by publishing its advertisement in the aviation industry journal EMA merely makes an 'invitation to treat': *Partridge v Crittenden* (1968). In other words, EMA's advertisement is an invitation to make a deal. It is quite safe for the business to make an 'invitation to treat' because, whatever the reply, the business could not be forced to sell. A response to an invitation to treat cannot result in a binding contract, therefore no contract between the parties has been formed at this stage. To reiterate, the main significance of an invitation to treat is that it is not an offer. Further analysis of the communications between the parties is necessary.

IS THERE AN OFFER AND IF SO BY WHICH PARTY?

Legal academic Treitel defines an offer as 'an expression of willingness to contract on certain terms, made with the intention that it shall become binding as soon as it is accepted by the person to whom it is addressed', the 'offeree'. Further, an offer is a statement of the terms on which the offeror is willing to be bound. An offer to buy can be written or spoken, or it can be inferred from the conduct of the offeror. At which point in the dealings between EMA and Zulu Aviation is an offer made and who makes the offer?

Whether two parties have an agreement or a valid offer is an issue which is determined by the court using the objective test (*Smith v Hughes* (1871)). Therefore the 'intention' referred to in the definition is objectively judged by the courts. In the English case of *Smith v Hughes* the court emphasised that the important thing is not a party's real intentions but how a reasonable person would view the situation. This is due mainly to common sense as each party would not wish to breach his side of the contract if it would make him or her culpable to damages. It would especially be contrary to the principle of certainty and clarity in commercial contract and the topic of mistake and how it affects the contract. As a minimum requirement the conditions for an offer should include at least the following four conditions: delivery date, price, terms of payment (that includes the date of payment) and detail description of the item on offer including a fair description of the condition or type of service. Without one of the minimum requirements of condition an offer of sale is not seen as a legal offer. Phil, of Zulu Aviation, communicates to Joseph verbally that he is considering purchasing the Airbus 321, but applying the Objective Test, he does not appear to use words that amount to an offer in law. Significantly, none of the four minimum requirements for an offer is discussed. Indeed, on the facts, he says that he wants to view the plane first, ostensibly before making a formal offer to purchase. This is because making an offer carries an element of risk in that if it is accepted Zulu Aviation would be legally bound to pay the agreed price (consideration). Accordingly, as no offer has been made by Phil to Joseph, no valid contract to purchase the Airbus exists between the parties.

However, what is the status of Phil stating to Joseph via telephone that he will pay £100,000 to EMA if it agrees not to sell the Airbus to another buyer for a period of five days? Do these facts amount to a legally binding contract between the parties? There appears to be an offer from Phil on objective terms in accordance with *Smith v Hughes* (1871). A reasonable person could state with certainty exactly what has been agreed. Note that Phil and Joseph, given the seniority of their positions within their respective organisations, would have the authority to negotiate on behalf of their organisations.

IS THERE VALID ACCEPTANCE OF PHIL'S OFFER?

As soon as an acceptance of an offer is received, a contract is created. The acceptance must be communicated: *Powell v Lee* (1908). Here, Joseph communicates clear and unequivocal acceptance to Phil verbally during the course of their telephone conversation. As soon as Joseph accepts Phil's offer, a contract comes into existence and both sides are legally bound by the terms of their agreement: *Entores Ltd v Miles Far East Corporation* (1955) (Court of Appeal). There do not appear to be any factors to vitiate the contract such as misrepresentation, mistake or duress on the facts.

IS THERE VALID CONSIDERATION?

The next issue is whether there is valid consideration. Consideration consists of a right given to one party, or a loss or detriment suffered by another. The consideration moving from Phil is the promise to pay £100,000. The consideration moving from EMA is the forbearance from selling the Airbus to another potential buyer. This amounts to valuable consideration according to the legal definition of consideration in *Currie v Misa* (1875). The £10,000 payment is known as 'executory consideration'. The consideration is called executory because when the contract between EMA and Zulu Aviation is made, Phil has not yet performed (executed) his £10,000 consideration.

PRESUMPTION OF INTENTION TO CREATE LEGAL RELATIONS

A contract will only be created if the parties appeared to intend to create a legal relationship. In the circumstances of the dealings between Phil and Joseph there is presumed intention to create legal relations as the agreement concerns a commercial matter between business people as opposed to a domestic or social matter: *Esso Petroleum Limited v Commissioners of Customs and Excise* (1976).

In conclusion, the offer and acceptance formula of contract law, developed in the nineteenth century, identifies a moment of formation when the parties are of one mind. Here, EMA's advertisement did not result in the formation of a contract between itself and Zulu Aviation for the sale of the Airbus. However, it is clear upon further analysis that there is nevertheless a legally binding contract between the parties, namely, EMA cannot sell the Airbus for the next five days to a third party or else it will be in breach of its promise to Zulu Aviation. Similarly, Zulu Aviation must pay EMA £100,000 for EMA's promise not to sell the Airbus to another buyer. The contract was formed via verbal telephone negotiations but is nevertheless still valid and binding on the parties. However, at this stage in the dealings there is no validly binding contract as regards the actual sale of the Airbus by EMA to Zulu Aviation.

Common Pitfalls ✗

Offer and acceptance analysis is a traditional approach in contract law used to determine whether an agreement exists between two parties. This is a typical contract law question that focuses on whether a contract of the sale/purchase of an Airbus has been made between the parties. Ensure that your answer addresses the specific concerns of EMA and Gunnell Aviation, rather than a general discussion of the law of contract.

Aim Higher ★

This question calls for effective deployment of the relevant case law at each point of the analysis. This will involve applying those cases to the specific facts of the scenario. Remember that there is no need to repeat the facts of the cases you cite; rather you should focus on the facts of the scenario and use the legal principles established by the case law as the legal authority for the conclusions you reach in your answer.

Consumer Law and the Tort of Negligence

INTRODUCTION

Under the tort of negligence everyone, including business people, owes a duty to other people in society not to act unreasonably and thereby cause them harm. If a person, or a legal person such as a company, causes harm to another by negligence, the injured person (the claimant) can recover compensation from the one who caused the harm (the defendant). A tort is a civil wrong, which is not a breach of contract. Liability in tort is not undertaken voluntarily. It is imposed by the courts, which have determined that certain types of behaviour will amount to a civil wrong, giving rise to tortious liability. Liability is based on fault, for example, dangerous driving causing an accident with another vehicle. The driver who drove dangerously without regard for the safety of others on the road is at fault and is therefore liable.

A classic definition of negligence states: 'negligence is the omission to do something which a reasonable man ... would do, or doing something which a prudent and reasonable man ... would not do.' In a legal action for negligence the claimant must prove three things:

1. Duty of care;
2. Breach of duty;
3. Damage caused by the breach.

First, in relation to the duty of care, the claimant must prove that the defendant owed him or her a duty of care. Generally, a duty of care is owed to anyone who one can reasonably foresee may be injured by one's act or omission. This was established in the most famous case in English law: the 'snail in the ginger-beer bottle case', *Donoghue v Stevenson* (1932).

Second, in relation to breach of duty, the standard of care required by law is one of reasonableness. If the defendant has acted reasonably, there is no breach of duty. The standard of care varies according to the danger. The greater the risk of more serious injury, the higher the standard of care owed, and thus the more that has to be done in order to have acted reasonably: *Latimer v AEC* and *Haley v LEB*.

Third, in relation to damage caused by the breach, this element of proof is usually referred to as causation. The claimant must prove on the balance of probabilities that the breach caused the damage that has been suffered. There are two stages in this:

(1) 'Causation in fact' – Was the injury a factual consequence of the breach, or did some other intervening factor actually cause the damage?
(2) 'Remoteness of damage' – The claimant can only recover for damage that is a reasonably foreseeable consequence of the breach, and not necessarily for all the damage caused.

This is basically a policy ruling. Many necessary activities in society would not take place if a person was to be wholly responsible for all the consequences of their actions, no matter how remote or unforeseeable: *The Wagon Mound* (1961) case. Although the damage must not be too remote, the defendant will be liable where the injury is more severe than one would reasonably have expected because of some peculiar susceptibility on the part of the claimant. This is known as the 'eggshell skull rule': *Smith v Leech Brain & Co.*

If the claimant succeeds in proving duty, breach and causation, the defendant may plead various defences to either avoid liability or reduce the amount of compensation payable. The two most important defences are:

(1) *Volenti non fit injuria* (to one who volunteers no harm is done). The defendant must prove that the claimant knew of and willingly consented to the risk. This defence is rare, particularly in employment cases, because it is difficult to show that the risk was willingly accepted: *Smith v Baker* (1891).
(2) Contributory negligence. If the claimant is partly to blame for the accident or for the increased severity of injuries, then the compensation will be reduced by the proportion by which the claimant is to blame, for example if no seat belt was worn in a car accident or no crash helmet in a motorbike accident.

Generally, it is not possible to recover damages for purely economic loss caused by negligence: *Weller Co v Foot and Mouth Disease Research Institute* (1966). However, economic loss directly consequent on physical damage CAN be recovered: *Spartan Steel v Martin* (1973); *Muirhead v Industrial Tank Specialities Ltd* (1985). An exception to this general rule applies in the case of negligent statements.

Since 1964, it has been accepted that financial loss caused by negligent statements *is* recoverable: *Hedley Byrne & Co v Heller and Partners Ltd* (1963). For this rule to apply there must be a special relationship between the parties. It is often very difficult to establish whether a sufficient relationship exists: *Caparo Industries Plc v Dickman* (1990). If a negligent statement of fact is made during the negotiation of a contract, the misled person may bring an action for negligent misrepresentation as well as for negligent misstatement: *Esso Petroleum Co Ltd v Mardon* (1976). This right arises from **s 2(1)** of the **Misrepresentation Act 1967**.

Consumer protection is particularly important to business, as manufacturers owe a duty of care to their customers. In 1985, the European Community introduced a Directive requiring all Member States to pass legislation to introduce the concept of product liability. The UK responded by passing the **Consumer Protection Act 1987**. As a result, where an unsafe product injures a person, s/he is able to sue the manufacturer (and perhaps others) without the need to prove the tort of negligence. This means that liability is strict and if the product is defective, the claimant does not need to prove fault. A defective product is one whose safety is not such as persons generally are entitled to expect (**s 3**). Damages may be claimed for either personal injury or death caused by the defective product: **s 5**. If the claimant somehow contributes to his or her injury, this can reduce the damages award. There are also several defences that can be raised under the Act.

QUESTION 32

Sean, a stockbroker, had invited Jane out for dinner for their first date. He made a booking with an award-winning and very expensive Italian restaurant – Gino's. They were getting along really well, the food was great, they shared a particularly good vintage of South African wine, and after the main course, Sean asked if Jane would like dessert. He was thrilled that she said yes as he likes a woman who will eat on a date. He ordered a cake and coffee for her, and chose chocolate ice cream for himself. As Jane was eating a mouthful of cake, she spluttered and coughed and spat out a decomposed insect. The sight of the decomposed insect caused her to suffer nervous shock and she collapsed. The restaurant bill cost £70, which Sean reluctantly paid in order to avoid any further embarrassment. Soon after, Sean took Jane home as she continued to feel ill. The contamination of the cake caused Jane to suffer gastroenteritis for several days. Both Jane and Sean were mortified at the turn of events and their potential romance did not recover. However, as they are both business people they decided to be practical and consider any remedy they may have against the restaurant.

▶ **Advise Sean and Jane.**

Answer Plan

The tort of negligence is the most important tort (other torts are negligent misstatement, occupier's liability, nuisance, trespass, defamation and vicarious liability). As such, it regularly features in business law examinations.

This is a typical problem question based on facts that are remarkably similar to the seminal negligence case, *Donoghue v Stevenson* (1932).

❖   Analyse the facts to hand in accordance with the three criteria: (1) the defendant owed Jane a duty of care; (2) the defendant breached that duty; and (3) a foreseeable type of damage was caused by the breach.

❖   Explain how the standard of care is assessed by an objective test laid down in *Blyth v Birmingham Waterworks* (1856).

❖   Discuss the concept of 'causation' and apply the 'but for' test illustrated in *Barnett v Chelsea & Kensington Hospital* (1968).

❖   Consider 'foreseeability' of damage as defined in *The Wagon Mound* (1961).

❖   Consider the effect of Jane's statutory rights, namely that she would also be able to rely on the **Consumer Protection Act 1987** without the need to prove negligence.

ANSWER

Before determining what remedies Sean and Jane may have against the restaurant Gino's, it is important to first establish Gino's liability as producer of the cake. The law of negligence or the **Consumer Protection Act 1987** governs this.

In establishing liability, it needs to be proven that:

(1)   The restaurant owed Jane a duty of care;
(2)   Gino's breached that duty; and
(3)   A foreseeable type of damage (nervous shock and gastroenteritis) was caused by the breach.

Fortunately, *Donoghue v Stevenson* (1932) (House of Lords), a case that created the foundation for the modern law of negligence, is a remarkably similar fact case. In *Donoghue*, it was established that manufacturers owe a duty of care to the ultimate consumers of their products and manufacturers should take reasonable steps to ensure that they do not injure their customers. As Lord Justice Atkin put it in his famous 'neighbour' speech, the Christian biblical rule that you should love thy neighbour became the law that you should not injure your neighbour. Who then, in the law, is a neighbour? Persons who are so closely and directly affected by your acts that you ought to reasonably have them in contemplation as being so affected when directing your mind to the acts or omissions that are called in question.

It is clear that Gino's restaurant owes Jane a duty of care even though Sean ordered and paid for the cake for her. In order to determine that Gino's has breached this duty, negligence needs to be proven. The standard of care is assessed by the 'objective' test established by Baron Alderson in the *Blyth v Birmingham Waterworks* (1856) case, which found that a water company was not negligent in allowing water to escape from its pipes. Baron Alderson stated:

> Negligence is the omission to do something, which a reasonable man, guided upon those considerations which ordinarily regulated the conduct of human affairs, would do, or doing something, which a prudent and reasonable man would not do. The standard demanded is thus not of perfection but of reasonableness. It is an objective standard taking no account of the defendant's incompetence – he may do the best he can and still be found negligent.

There is no question that it is reasonable to expect Gino's to provide customers with an insect-free piece of cake.

In order to establish the causation of damage, Jane must prove that harm would not have occurred 'but for' the negligence of the defendant. This test was a creation of Lord Denning. The test is best illustrated by *Barnett v Chelsea & Kensington Hospital* (1968) and *Robinson v Post Office* (1974). In the former, a patient who visited a hospital suffering from vomiting was negligently turned away by the doctor and died from arsenic poisoning. As the patient would have died anyway, whether or not he had received treatment, the hospital was found not liable for the patient's death. In Jane's case, but for eating the decomposed insect that lay hidden in the cake, she would not have suffered nervous shock or gastroenteritis. There does not appear, on the facts, to be any other cause for the gastroenteritis.

Further, in order for Jane to claim a loss, the loss must have been a type of loss or injury that was a foreseeable consequence of Gino's breach of duty of care. The loss must not be too remote: *The Wagon Mound* (1961). If the personal injury/damage is foreseeable, the exact consequences need not be foreseeable. It is reasonable to conclude that the type of damage that would ensue from eating cake contaminated with a decomposed insect would result in nervous shock and gastroenteritis. Damages can be awarded for psychiatric injury, known as 'nervous shock'; however, the courts are cautious in awarding damages for nervous shock.

In summary, Jane has a strong case for holding Gino's liable for her injury as they made the cake on the premises. Therefore she can sue the restaurant for damages even though Sean ordered and paid for the cake. Jane can claim pecuniary (monetary) damages as a result of her personal injury. Her remedy will be monetary as this is the best way to compensate her, as much as money can do for the suffering.

Note that as the cake was 'unsafe', Jane would also be able to rely on the **Consumer Protection Act 1987** to sue Gino's without proving negligence. **Section 5** of the Act allows a claimant to claim damages for death or any personal injury caused by a defective product. However, these new rights to sue do not detract at all from the common-law negligence principles set out in *Donoghue v Stevenson* (1932), which is thought to be one of the most important cases in the history of English law.

Common Pitfalls ✘

Read each sentence of the fact scenario carefully. Discuss the tort law issues relating to liability. A detailed application of the key case law, *Donoghue v Stevenson* (1932), which in effect created the modern law of negligence, is warranted here as it is a case directly in point; in other words, the facts are remarkably similar.

Aim Higher ★

Ensure you consider the point of view of the client you are advising, in this case the victim Jane and Sean who paid the restaurant bill. Really, the victim of the tort is Jane. What outcome does she want? Identify the corresponding legal issues. In other words, what sort of legal argument needs to be advanced in order for Jane to obtain financial compensation for her injury and suffering? Work your way through the various tort law issues as they arise in the question, interchangeably stating the legal principle and how this might apply to the facts. Conclude by stating the possible outcome(s), in other words whether the restaurant is liable.

QUESTION 33

Angelina approached Christian Auctioneers to give her a free valuation of some antique furniture that she had recently inherited from her grandmother and was considering selling at auction. Christian sent their employee Brad, a furniture expert, to provide the valuation at Angelina's flat.

Having had the furniture valued, Angelina asked Brad how much a painting that she had also inherited was worth. Brad, who had been instructed by Christian not to give advice outside his field of expertise, looked at the painting and pronounced it to be of little value, adding, 'I may not know much about art but I know what I like – and it's not this!'

Shortly afterwards Angelina sold the painting privately for £100 to an elderly neighbour who thought it would look fantastic in her sitting room. A few weeks later, Angelina read the following headline in her local paper: 'Pensioner hits jackpot with rare Rembrandt for £100!' The painting that Angelina had sold was pictured underneath. Advise Angelina whether she has any rights and remedies against Brad and Christian in connection with the incorrect advice given to her about the painting.

Answer Plan

This is a fairly complex problem question on the subject of tortious liability for negligent misstatement.

* Define and explain the tort of negligent misstatement with reference to the House of Lords' decision in *Hedley Byrne v Heller* (1963).
* Consider the viability of Angelina's claim for pure economic loss by applying the criteria established in *Hedley Byrne v Heller* to this fact situation.
* As Brad is probably impecunious (cash poor), consider whether Christian Auctioneers, as Brad's employer, should be vicariously liable for the advice.

ANSWER

It has long been recognised that liability in tort might arise from negligent actions, but liability for negligent misstatements and negligent advice has been less well accepted by the courts. A negligent misstatement might be defined as a representation of fact, carelessly made, which is relied on by the claimant to his or her disadvantage. Whether Angelina has a strong civil case against Brad and/or Christian Auctioneers for the tort of negligent misstatement will need to be carefully assessed because the burden of proof lies with Angelina to prove all the required elements of the tort on the balance of probabilities. Angelina has sold the painting at a serious undervalue. Would she be successful in claiming this purely economic loss?

At law, liability in tort for negligent misstatement was first seriously considered by the House of Lords in *Hedley Byrne & Co Ltd v Heller and Partners Ltd* (1963) (House of Lords). In this case, the claimant advertising agency sought to recover its economic losses from the defendant bank on the grounds that the bank had negligently overstated the financial resources of one of the agency's clients. It was generally accepted by the House of Lords that, in principle, a person who gives inaccurate information, where it is reasonably foreseeable that it will be acted on, could be liable for losses suffered as a result of that reliance. This decision is little more than a broad interpretation of *Donoghue v Stevenson* (1932) – the 'neighbour principle' applies where there is a 'special relationship' between the claimant and the defendant. The claimants in *Hedley Byrne* failed, not because their losses were unrecoverable in law, but because they had not shown that their reliance on the defendant's 'without prejudice' statement was reasonable.

The decision in *Hedley Byrne* was not really concerned with pure economic loss, but with liability for statements. However, by recognising that there are some circumstances in which pure economic loss is recoverable, *Hedley Byrne* did pave the way for a rapid expansion in litigation for economic loss. As a result, when looking at the cases that followed *Hedley Byrne*, and which did not impose liability, it is not always easy to determine whether the court's decision was influenced more by a desire to limit liability for economic loss than for reasons related to negligent misstatement.

In relation to Angelina, she may very well be able to recover for pure economic loss, provided she can prove not just negligence *simpliciter* (i.e. duty of care, breach, and causation: *Donoghue v Stevenson*), but also the criteria (*obiter*) in *Hedley Byrne v Heller*. In summary, the criteria are that there must be: (i) a special relationship between the parties; (ii) an assumption of responsibility; and (iii) reasonable reliance on the advice by Angelina.

In relation to (i), a special relationship will arise only if Angelina could reasonably and foreseeably expect to be able to rely on Brad's advice. There is no requirement that Brad should receive anything in return for the advice. However, it is necessary for Angelina to ask for the advice. The advice should be given in a business setting – here, given that the initial purpose of Brad's visit was to give advice on the furniture, this is provable, even though the meeting took place at Angelina's home.

Did Brad assume responsibility for his advice? A key fact is that Brad's advice came with a quasi-disclaimer: 'I may not know much about art....' Further, there was no serious attempt by Brad to examine the painting and thus give meaningful advice. These factors may serve to get Brad and his employer Christian Auctioneers off the hook and make them not liable for negligent misstatement.

Was it reasonable for Angelina to rely on Brad's advice concerning the painting? It is probably unlikely that a reasonable person would have thought an expert in antique furniture would also know about paintings.

The court will also consider the ratio in *Caparo v Dickman* (1990) when it assesses whether it would be 'fair, just and reasonable' to impose liability on Brad and Christian Auctioneers. Here, the court probably will not impose liability, given that the trend since *Caparo* is to reduce the circumstances when liability will arise.

If, however, the court were to think otherwise, Brad would be primarily liable. Unfortunately, it is highly unlikely that he would have the money to satisfy a claim; that is, the difference in value between £100 and a rare Rembrandt! Consequently, Angelina should join Christian Auctioneers to the action to try to hold them vicariously liable. Employers such as Christian are vicariously liable for torts committed by their employees (e.g. Brad) during the course of their employment. Note that employers must be insured for the torts of their employees committed in the course of their employment: **Employers' (Compulsory Insurance) Act 1969**.

Christian Auctioneers may try to negate vicarious liability given that they instructed Brad 'not to give advice outside his field of expertise'. An employer who absolutely prohibits an employee from performing certain acts will generally not be liable if the employee ignores the prohibition. However, if the employer only prohibits the manner in which an authorised act should be performed, the employer will remain liable for the acts of its employees. In *Iqbal v London Transport Executive* (1973), a bus conductor had been expressly prohibited from driving buses. The bus on which he worked was parked in such a way that it was causing an obstruction. The conductor was ordered to get a colleague to move the bus, but he decided to move it himself, causing an accident. It was held that the employer was not vicariously liable for the acts of its employee. Accordingly, it is most likely that Christian Auctioneers would not be made vicariously liable. This means that, although Angelina will have established a case for pure economic loss as a result of Brad's negligent misstatement, she will be without a remedy.

Common Pitfalls ✗

Do not treat a problem question as an invitation to write an abstract essay about the legal issues involved in the problem. The facts are all important and application to the facts is essential. Students will frequently write out all the law they consider to be raised by the facts and then, without separating the issues clearly, leave their application to the end. The dangers of excessive repetition and irrelevant points of law are high and this is very poor legal style.

QUESTION 34

Zulu Aviation Ltd has experienced the following incidents:

(a) Martin, a cargo pilot employed by Zulu Aviation, sustained severe head and leg injuries while landing a plane which overran the runway due to a failure involving the plane's brakes. In the investigation following the accident, the report concluded that Zulu Aviation Ltd had not upgraded the brake system in accordance with the required aircraft maintenance schedule, presumably to reduce costs.

(b) Cargo comprising 300 laptop computers, owned by Laptops R Us, was irreparably damaged in the incident and is no longer in saleable condition.

▶ Advise Zulu Aviation Ltd of any liability it might have to Martin or Laptops R Us. Refer to relevant case law to support your answer.

Answer Plan

This question raises many issues of tort law and in particular the law of negligence and compensation for losses, namely personal injury and damage to property.

❖ Introduce the general area of law that will govern the legal advice required by this problem question.
❖ Next, identify the type of injury or loss that arises from the plane overrunning the runway (note there is personal injury and damage to property).
❖ Analyse Zulu Aviation's liability to Martin for personal injury.
❖ Analyse Zulu Aviation's liability to Laptops R Us for damage to their computers (the cargo).

ANSWER

The focus of the question is the law of tort, in particular negligence and compensation for losses, namely personal injury and damage to property.

(A)   LIABILITY TO MARTIN FOR PERSONAL INJURY

Every employer has a duty to provide safe plant, appliances, premises and system of work. In this instance, the plane would be regarded in law as Martin's place of work. However, merely owing a duty of care is not enough to give rise to liability for the tort of negligence. Zulu Aviation will only be liable to its employee Martin, if they can be shown, on the balance of probabilities, to have breached the duty of care owed: *Donoghue v Stevenson* (1932) (House of Lords). This is an objective standard. An employee such as Martin who is injured by his employer's breach of a duty of care can sue in the tort of negligence.

As a result of not upgrading the plane's brakes, Zulu Aviation have fallen below the standard of care owed to employee pilots and will face civil liability for breaching their common-law duty to provide their employee Martin with safe working conditions, plant and equipment: *Bradford v Robinson Rentals* (1967). The likelihood of harm to Martin was very considerable and the cost of making sure the accident did not happen was reasonable: *Paris v Stepney Borough Council* (1951) (House of Lords). There is no suggestion in the facts that Martin contributed to his injuries by mishandling the plane on landing.

As Martin is able to show that the defective plane brakes caused his personal injuries he is likely to be successful in his action for compensation against his employer. Martin will be able to claim pecuniary losses and non-pecuniary losses. Damages in respect of pain and suffering, loss of amenity (loss of ability to enjoy life), loss of earnings and the costs of health care are also recoverable.

Martin will be expected to take reasonable steps to mitigate his loss. This means that Martin has the legal obligation to minimise the effects and losses resulting from the injury. The duty to mitigate works to deny recovery of any part of damages that could have been reasonably avoided. 'Reasonably avoided' has no specific definition, but generally means what a reasonable person would do under similar circumstances. For practical purposes this means that Martin would not be able to recover for any harm which he could have avoided if he had sought adequate medical care. The reason the court requires the injured party to seek medical care is to try to keep damages to a minimum. For example, if a person steps on a nail, but by the time they seek medical attention six months later, they need to have their foot amputated, the injured person wouldn't be able to obtain the same type of damages as someone whose injury is more immediate. In summary, damages will not be recoverable in respect of losses which the claimant brought upon by himself by his own careless actions after the tort had been committed by the defendant.

Turning to Zulu Aviation, the firm may face potential criminal liability under the **Health and Safety at Work Act 1974. Section 2(1)** of the Act states that it shall be the duty of every employer to ensure, so far as is reasonably practicable, the health, safety and welfare at work of all his employees.

(B)   LIABILITY TO LAPTOPS R US FOR DAMAGE TO PROPERTY

The same set of facts gives rise to damage to commercial property. Is damage to property treated differently to personal injury? In respect of goods, the measure of damages will ordinarily be the cost of restoration of the goods. This cost will generally be assessed by reference to the market value. A claim might also be made for loss of the use of the goods if replacement goods could not easily be obtained. Such a claim could take account of profit lost on account of the goods not being available.

Common Pitfalls   ✗

In relation to the cargo contract between Zulu Aviation and Laptops R Us, avoid the temptation to speculate on the existence of an exclusion clause as no facts are presented in the scenario to suggest that an exclusion clause existed (even though one may well exist in a real-life scenario).

Aim Higher   ★

To score a top mark, a student needs to demonstrate a thorough knowledge of the law combined with strong legal analysis skills and a superior ability to express themselves coherently and logically in written form. Strong answers display a discussion of the legal principles accompanied by authority, namely a reference to relevant supporting case law or statute. Often, students are better able to cite case law authority than statutory authority. In this problem question, to achieve top marks students need to refer to BOTH types of primary law.

Sole Traders, Partnerships and Business Names

INTRODUCTION

An important decision for business people to make is to decide what legal form the business will take. The legal form chosen is not irrevocable, but it will take time and money to undo mistakes. There are four main types:

1. Sole trader;
2. Partnership;
3. Limited liability partnership (LLP), available since 2001; and
4. Limited company.

In this chapter, we will focus on the first three legal structures listed above.

SOLE TRADER

A sole trader, or proprietor, is someone who trades alone and bears the full responsibility for the actions of the business. The other way to work alone is using a limited company, which will be discussed in the next chapter. A sole tradership is the simplest and cheapest form of business structure to establish and has the maximum flexibility. Legal and set-up costs are lower than for other business structures and governmental control is minimal compared with partnerships and companies. A sole trader simply has to register with the Inland Revenue within three months of starting up and notify HM Revenue & Customs. A sole trader will need to decide whether to register for value-added tax (VAT). A sole proprietor takes all the net profits and to wind up the business costs nothing.

However, carrying on business as a sole trader does have its disadvantages, the major one being that the sole trader is liable for taxation as an individual. S/he is required to declare income and pay tax at the personal rate, which could be up to 40 per cent. It can also be difficult to raise finance for this type of business to grow, and profitability depends on the actions and the good health of the owner. A key disadvantage is also the fact that a sole trader is liable for all the business's debts (liability is unlimited). The sole trader's personal assets, such as the family home, car, furniture and so forth, can be seized to pay the business's debts, and if the debts are particularly onerous the sole trader could become bankrupt.

PARTNERSHIP

A partnership is a relationship between people carrying on business in common with a view to a profit. The formation of a partnership is relatively inexpensive and simple to establish. Although a written partnership agreement is not required to start the partnership, and an oral agreement is still legally binding, it is sensible to draw up a partnership agreement to ensure the business is carried on in a way that suits the partners. Standard forms of partnership agreements are available for sale from legal stationers, so it is not necessary to write one from scratch. Nevertheless, it is advisable to ensure that a qualified solicitor reviews the final draft.

There are four main characteristics that distinguish a partnership from other forms of business:

1. The legal system identifies the individual partners of the business and not the partnership firm.
2. Each partner has unlimited legal liability for: (a) the debts of the firm as a whole; (b) taxes; and (c) the actions of the other partners.
3. Each partner's interest in the firm is non-transferable.
4. Each partner has a right to take part in the management of the firm.

However, a properly planned partnership can form a satisfying, profitable and lasting business for those involved.

LIMITED LIABILITY PARTNERSHIP (LLP)

The new form of limited liability partnership (LLP) may give an air of credibility to a business venture as it means that the business must meet certain commitments at Companies House, which regulates LLPs and limited companies. An LLP has a separate legal identity and can be formed by completing an incorporation document (Form LL IN01), paying a fee and registering a name at Companies House. There must be at least two directors who will be responsible for getting the accounts audited and sending an annual return to Companies House, which will be available to the public. There are penalties if the LLP's accounts are filed late and potential fines range from £100 to £1,000.

The concept of limited liability is an attractive feature of the LLP and shareholders' liability for debt is, in most cases, limited to the amount they paid for the LLP shares. The personal assets of the directors can only be touched if the LLP has been trading fraudulently or when the directors knew it was insolvent.

Finally, it is important for a business to select a business name that complies with the **Business Name Act 1985 (BNA 1985)**. However, business names are no longer registered under the **Companies Act 2006**, or with any government department. The **BNA 1985** gives the Secretary of State certain control over the name a business can choose and what must be disclosed to the public about the ownership of the business.

QUESTION 35

What is the most appropriate business structure for the following business people?

(a) Three close university friends who have recently qualified as dentists;
(b) An up-and-coming portrait artist;
(c) A group of 35 accountants who recently met during a networking event who wish to establish a boutique accounting practice aimed at professional sportspeople.

Answer Plan

This is a subdivided question. Answer (a) to (c) in turn in alphabetical order. Unless you are told otherwise, it is reasonable for you to assume that each section carries equal marks. This means that each section is worth 33 per cent and you should allocate equal time to each subsection. The purpose of this question is to assess the student's knowledge of the three forms of business structure – the sole trader, the partnership and the limited liability partnership.

❖ Discuss the practicalities of what is involved to set up the appropriate structure and note any governing legislation.
❖ Consider the advantages and disadvantages of the recommended structure in light of the facts.

ANSWER

An important decision to make early on in the process of planning a new business is what legal form the business will take. This decision is not irrevocable, but it will take time and money to undo mistakes. One can choose to set up as a sole trader, partnership, limited liability partnership or a limited company. [NB However, company law will be covered in Chapter 10.]

(a) In this situation, concerning the most appropriate form of business structure for three professional dentists, a partnership is the recommended route. A partnership is defined by s 1(1) of the **Partnership Act 1890 (PA)** as 'the relation which subsists between persons carrying on a business in common with a view of profit'.

The formation of a partnership is relatively inexpensive and simple to establish. Although a written agreement is not required to begin a partnership and an oral agreement is still legally binding, it is prudent to either purchase a standard form of partnership agreement from a legal stationer or incur a fee for a solicitor to draft a tailor-made agreement, which is more expensive.

The two most important characteristics of a partnership are: (1) the unlimited liability of the partners; and (2) the power of partners to act as agents of their fellow partners. If the three dentists entered into a partnership, they would not be protected by limited liability (i.e. limited to what they each invested in the business) because a partnership is not a legal person and has no separate legal identity. The partners would each act as the agents of their fellow partners. This means that the firm is liable for a partner's torts on contracts entered into. Other characteristics include the non-transferability of the partners' interests and the right of each partner to take part in the management.

Partners are in a fiduciary position to each other. The concept of a 'fiduciary' means that partners are more than contracting parties – they are expected to behave towards each other as if they were trustees for each other, making full disclosure and being scrupulously fair in their dealings. **Sections 28–30** of the **PA 1890** spell out three specific 'fiduciary' or 'higher' duties: (1) partners must render true accounts and information; (2) they must account for profits; and (3) they must not compete with the firm. The provisions are all based on principles established by the courts in connection with fiduciaries.

When the firm is wound up, the partnership property will be used to pay the debts and liabilities of the firm. For example, if partnership property increases in value, this increase will belong to the firm rather than to any individual partner. Also, partnership property should be used exclusively for the purposes of the partnerships.

Many professionals have traditionally practised in partnerships, but there are some disadvantages to the structure to be taken into consideration. Each partner is legally bound by the actions – responsible or otherwise – of the other members. Personality clashes may occur or an individual's financial difficulties could affect the partnership. Each partner has unlimited liability for the debts of the business. Nevertheless, a properly planned partnership can form a satisfying, profitable and lasting business for those involved.

(b) A portrait artist primarily works on his or her own. In the field of portraiture, this seems sensible; the choice is either to set up as a sole trader or as a limited company.

It is very easy and straightforward to set up as a sole trader or a limited company. We will focus on why an artist would prefer to set up as a sole trader.

As a sole trader, the artist would bear full responsibility for the business. It is the simplest and cheapest form of business structure to establish and has the maximum flexibility. This would probably appeal to an 'up-and-coming' or 'struggling' artist. From a practical point of view, a sole trader needs to register for national insurance with HM Customs & Revenue by completing form SA1. A small fine is set for sole traders who fail to register within three months from the end of the month in which the business starts. Another advantage is that governmental control is minimal when compared with partnerships or companies. The proprietor takes all the profits and to wind up the business costs nothing.

However, trading as a sole trader does have its disadvantages, the major one being that the sole trader is liable for taxation as an individual. One is required to declare the income from the business and this income is taxed at the personal rate, which can be in excess of 40p in the pound. It can also be difficult to raise finance for the business to grow. The profitability of the business depends on the actions and good health of the owner. Nevertheless, many artists feel that operating as a sole trader is their preferred form of legal business structure.

(c) What is contemplated in this case is a large partnership with over thirty members who wish to practise accountancy in a sports context. Since April 2000, it has been possible for two or more persons to trade together as a limited liability partnership (LLP). An LLP is a separate legal person and a corporate body in its own right. An LLP is liable for its own debts; it can have perpetual succession (this overcomes the issue of a partnership having to dissolve on the death of a partner) and can own property and enter into contracts, can sue and can be sued. However, the members of LLPs are taxed as individuals on their share of the firm's profits; they do not pay corporate tax.

The process for forming an LLP involves incorporation by registration with the Registrar of Companies. LLPs do not have directors and shareholders; rather they have members and designated members. Every LLP must have at least one designated member. The designated member has more onerous duties as an officer of the firm as they must sign the accounts and the annual return, and liaise with Companies House regarding the names of designated members.

Two key advantages of an LLP business structure for the group of accountants is that first, although every member is an agent of the LLP and enters into contracts on behalf of the firm, the LLP is not bound if the member in fact had no authority to make the particular contract and the third party either knew this or did not believe that the member was a member of the LLP. Second, any member of an LLP can petition the court for minority protection, that is, claiming unfair prejudice under **s 459** of the **Companies Act 1985** or to wind up the LLP under **s 122** of the **Insolvency Act 1986**.

A disadvantage of an LLP is that it cannot raise capital by selling shares to people who have no desire to manage the business.

As the group of accountants, as professionals, will usually desire to be involved in the management of the firm, the LLP structure is appealing because they will each acquire management rights as well as a significant degree of limited liability over a traditional partnership.

Common Pitfalls ✖

Avoid a general answer on business structures. At each point put yourself in the position of the dentists, artist and group of accountants and consider what type of legal business structure is the optimum for that particular form of business.

Aim Higher ★

Aim to evaluate the norm in terms of legal business structure in each of the professions and why this is the case.

QUESTION 36

Jennifer and Josie have recently graduated as dentists and completed their professional exams. They wish to set up a dental practice and realise it is prudent to draft a formal partnership agreement to govern their relationship. What are the 'universal' matters that all formal written partnership agreements are likely to deal with?

Answer Plan

This essay question is aimed at having the students reflect on the issues arising when two or more people carry on business together in partnership with a view to a profit. As a partnership is a contractual relationship, it is important to express the rules that will govern these issues and the obligations of each party in writing, despite the fact that the **Partnership Act 1890** does not require a written partnership agreement.

❖ Define a partnership under the **Partnership Act 1890**.
❖ Clarify that a partnership has no separate legal identity.
❖ List the 'universal matters' commonly found in a partnership agreement.
❖ Recommend additional matters in order to tailor the agreement.

ANSWER

Jennifer and Josie are contemplating setting a dental practice and have determined to enter in a partnership arrangement. **Section 1** of the **Partnership Act 1890 (PA 1890)** states that 'partnership is the relationship which subsists between persons carrying on a business in common with a view to a profit'. A partnership has no separate legal personality apart from its members in the way a company does.

There are no specific legal requirements governing the formation of a partnership. Partnerships arise from the agreement of the parties involved and are governed by the general principles of contract law. This means that a partnership is only created if all of the requirements of a contract are fulfilled. There must be an offer, an acceptance, and an intention to create legal relations and consideration. The **PA 1890** tends to serve as a default where the partners do not provide for their own operation.

What legal obligations will the partners have that should be documented? In this instance, Jennifer and Josie wish to document the operation of their proposed partnership by way of a formal partnership agreement (articles of partnership). The partnership agreement will be an internal document for use by the partners to manage their relationship. There are several key matters that would normally be dealt with by almost any formal partnership agreement, which are known as 'universal' articles. These are summarised below:

❖ 'The parties to the agreement' – In *Saywell v Pope* (1979) it was shown that the final decision as to whether or not a person is a partner can only be made in the light of all of the evidence. It should also be realised that the fact that a person is not included in the agreement as a partner will not prevent him or her from being liable as a partner.
❖ 'The nature of the business' – First, this is important because **s 5** of the **PA 1890** makes partners agents of the firm and of their fellow partners for the purposes of the firm's business, but not for other purposes. Second, **s 30** imposes a fiduciary

duty preventing partners from carrying on a business that competes with the business of the firm or is of the same nature as the business of the firm.

❖ 'The name of the firm' – First, the name must comply with the requirements of the **Business Names Act 1985**. Second, the name must not be designed to deceive the public by causing confusion with another business. Third, **s 34** of the **Companies Act 1985** makes it a criminal offence for a partnership to use the word 'Limited' or 'Ltd' in its name.

❖ 'Dates of commencement and dissolution' – The date at which a partnership commences is a matter of fact, which will be determined by examining all of the evidence. However, the fact that a partnership agreement states a date of commencement is likely to be very strong evidence of a partnership having existed from that date.

❖ 'The capital of the firm and of the individual partners' – **Section 24(1)** of the **PA 1890** provides that: 'All the partners are entitled to share equally in the capital and the profits of the business, and must contribute equally towards the losses, whether of capital or otherwise sustained by the firm.' This presumption is commonly varied in the partnership agreement. In many partnerships one partner provides the capital while the other provides the skills.

❖ 'The salary and profit entitlement of the partners' – Very commonly, partners do not share equally in the profits of the firm.

❖ 'The management of the business' – **Section 24(5)** of the **PA 1890** states that: 'Every partner may take part in the management of the partnership business.' **Section 24** of the **PA** applies only if no contrary agreement is expressly or impliedly made. The partnership agreement should set out the duties of the various partners, how majority decisions should be taken, and whether or not some of the partners are excluded from the right to do certain things.

❖ 'Banking arrangements and the right to draw cheques' – The agreement should name the firm's bank and specify whether or not individual partners have the right to draw cheques on the partnership account. It is commonly agreed that the signatures of two partners are required on cheques to the value of more than a specified amount.

❖ 'The firm's accounts' – The agreement will generally state that the firm's accounts are to be drawn up on certain dates.

❖ 'Admission and expulsion of partners' – The agreement should set out the grounds on which a partner can be expelled from the partnership and when new partners can be admitted. If there is no express or implied agreement to the contrary, a new partner can only be admitted by the consent of all of the existing partners (**s 24(7)**).

❖ 'Death or retirement of partners' – **Section 33(1)** provides that the death of a partner dissolves the firm unless the partners agree otherwise. It would be usual in a commercial firm for the partnership agreement to state that the firm should be carried on after the death of a partner, and to provide a right for a partner to retire from the firm after giving the stated period of notice.

❖ 'Valuation of goodwill' – The agreement should set out how the goodwill should be valued and the entitlement, in respect of the goodwill, of partners who die or retire.

❖ 'Arbitration' – A dispute resolution clause is always recommended to deal with internal problems.

Additional matters that Jennifer and Josie should consider including in the agreement are: place of business, provision for increase of capital, return of capital, loans by partners, duties of partners, private obligations of partners, accountants and tax agents, prohibitions, holidays, insurance (sickness, life), and dissolution or winding-up. There may be more!

Common Pitfalls ✘

Since the decision to enter into a partnership has been taken, there is no need to consider the advantages and disadvantages of a corporation in answering this question.

Aim Higher ★

Aim to address the specific concerns of the partnership, Jennifer and Josie, in a small business between friends. In other words, ensure you tailor the legal advice.

QUESTION 37

What are the legal requirements for a sole trader or a partnership in choosing a business name? What if another business is already using the name?

Answer Plan

This is an essay question designed to require the student to consider the issues that arise when selecting a name for a sole trader or partnership.

❖ Consider if there is a need to register a business name and what preliminary checks should be made.

❖   Note any legislation that may govern business names.
❖   Note any prohibitions under relevant legislation.
❖   What options are there if another business is already using the preferred name?

ANSWER

A person can trade under their own name, or choose a different business name. A business name is a name used by any person, partnership or company for carrying on business, unless it is the same as their own name. Sole traders, for example, often use their own surname. A partnership can trade under the names of all the partners or a business name. Partners commonly choose to be known by their collective surnames, although they can in general choose to be known by any other name. A limited company or LLP can trade under its registered name or use a different business name.

There is a register of company names and LLP names, but there is no central registry of partnership names. The choice of a suitable business name involves two important legal considerations. First, although business names are not registered under the **Companies Act 2006**, some of the rules included in that Act in sections 1192 to 1199 do apply, principally:

❖   Restrictions on the use of certain words in the name and names that could imply a connection with a government department or public body;
❖   Inappropriate and misleading use of a name ending, e.g. 'limited' at the end of the name;
❖   Rules requiring the names of sole traders and partnerships using a business name to be displayed on stationery and signs at business premises.

Second, the name must not be designed to deceive the public by causing confusion with another business.

PRELIMINARY CHECKS

Before choosing a business name, there are a few preliminary checks that need to be made. First, one should check the WebCheck service at Companies House to ensure the chosen name is not the 'same as' an existing name on the index of company names. What words and expressions will be regarded as the 'same as'? When comparing one name with another, certain words and expressions will be regarded as the 'same as', for example, 'and' and '&', 'plus' and '+', '1' and 'one', '£' and 'pound', '%' and 'per cent', and '@' and 'at'. In relation to 'same as' names, 'Aerospace Limited' is the 'same as': Aero Space Limited, Aerospace UK Limited, Aerospace.co.uk PLC, Aerospace International Ltd and Aerospace Services Public Limited Company.

Second, check the Trade Marks Register of the UK Intellectual Property Office to ensure that the proposed name does not infringe an existing trade mark. Third, to check web domain names free of charge, search at a name registration service such as www.netnames.co.uk.

SENSITIVE WORDS AND EXPRESSIONS

Section 1193 of the **Companies Act 2006** makes it a criminal offence to use certain names unless the written approval of the Secretary of State for Trade and Industry is granted. About 100 words are specified including, among others: 'authority', 'charity', 'chartered', 'dental', 'institute', 'nursing', 'police', 'Royal' and 'society'. Using one of these words without authorisation could constitute a criminal offence. The Act gives the Secretary of State certain control over business names and what you must disclose to others about the ownership of the business. For example, controlled words include 'bank', 'banker', 'banking' or 'deposit', the use of which will require authorisation from the Financial Services Authority (FSA). Other names that need approval include names that give the impression that a business is connected with Her Majesty's Government, the Scottish or Welsh administrations, or a local authority. These names must be approved by the Secretary of State and may require support from the appropriate government department or relevant body. The Secretary of State is also required to approve the use of a name that could mislead the public into believing that a business has a size or status that is not justified.

Sensitive words as set out in the Act, which imply national or international pre-eminence, such as 'British', 'England', 'English', 'Scotland', 'Scottish', 'Wales', 'Welsh', 'Ireland', 'Irish', 'National', 'Great Britain', 'United Kingdom', 'European' and 'International', among others, need to be carefully considered. The business will need to apply for approval to use the 'sensitive' words in its business name.

Despite the offence created by **ss 1192–1197** a business is permitted to carry on using a name which had been lawful under the **Business Names Act 1985**. It also allows a person who has taken over a business to carry on using such a name for 12 months after the transfer.

DISCLOSURE

If a business trades under any name other than a personal name or a registered business name it must disclose the ownership of the business and an official address on its stationery, on a sign at its premises, on its website (if it has one) and to any business contact who asks for it (**ss 1200–1208 Companies Act 2006**).

Additional protection for a business name may be gained by registering it as a trade mark or as a domain.

Finally, if anyone else is using the proposed business name, consider the circumstances. If a sole trader at the other end of the country is using it, there may not be a problem. However, if another local business or national firm were using it, it would be wise to choose a different name in order to avoid causing confusion to the public or to incur the risk of an action for passing off from the rival business.

Common Pitfalls ✗

Avoid discussing your own personal experience with business names or ventures you may be planning. A legal discussion is required.

Aim Higher ★

Focus on the law relating to the selection, use and protection of a business name.

Company Law

INTRODUCTION

Company law concerns the study of registered companies under the **Companies Act 2006**. As the most common form of commercial organisation in the Western world, knowledge of what companies actually are, how they operate and the law relating to them is of prime importance to business people. Interestingly, over 90 per cent of companies registered in the United Kingdom are classified as small companies.

CHARACTERISTICS OF LIMITED COMPANIES

A company is a separate legal entity (or legal person) for most purposes. Companies are treated, in effect, as artificial persons when registered under the statute. As such, a company can sue or be sued in their own name, enter into and enforce contracts, hold title to and transfer property and be found civilly and criminally liable for breaches of the law. Because a company cannot be imprisoned, the usual criminal penalty is the assessment of a fine or other sanction. Companies have several unique characteristics, including the following:

LIMITED LIABILITY OF SHAREHOLDERS

As separate legal entities, companies are liable for their own debts. The shareholders have only limited liability, which means that they are liable only to the extent of their capital contribution (investment) and do not have liability for the company's debts.

FREE TRANSFERABILITY OF SHARES

Company shares are personal property that is freely transferable by the shareholder by sale, assignment or gift. Shareholders in a private company may agree among themselves on restrictions on transfer of shares. National markets, such as the London Stock Exchange, were developed for the organised sale of securities to the public.

PERPETUAL EXISTENCE

Companies exist in perpetuity unless a specific duration is stated in the company's constitution. The company can, however, be voluntarily wound up by the shareholders or involuntarily wound up by the company's unpaid creditors if the court grants their petition for bankruptcy.

CENTRALISED MANAGEMENT

The board of directors makes policy decisions regarding company operations. The shareholders appoint directors. The directors in turn appoint company officers and employees to run the company's day-to-day operations. Together, the directors and officers form the company management.

CORPORATE GOVERNANCE

Corporate governance is the system by which companies are directed and controlled. It concerns the relationship between the constituent parts of a company: the directors, the board (and its subcommittees) and the shareholders.

Transparency and accountability are the most important elements of good corporate governance. This includes:

❖ The timely provision by companies of good-quality information;
❖ A clear and credible company decision-making process;
❖ Shareholders giving proper consideration to the information provided and making considered judgments.

As a company is no more than a vehicle for facilitating and regulating the carrying on of business activities, it should defer to modern economic and social needs. As those needs change, so the rules and, more importantly, the practices of company law change.

All limited companies in the UK are registered at Companies House, an Executive Agency of the Department of Trade and Industry. There are more than 2.5 million limited companies registered in Great Britain and 400,550 new companies were incorporated in 2010.

QUESTION 38

What role do the principles of separate corporate personality and limited liability play in relation to companies?

Answer Plan

This essay question focuses on two key issues:

(1)   Separate corporate personality; and
(2)   Limited liability.

It is essential that the students address both these concepts and it is reasonable to assume the discussion of each concept will carry roughly equal marks. This means that the discussion of each concept is worth 50 per cent and you should allocate equal time to each subsection.

❖   Examine the nature of a company and assess the essential characteristics that companies possess.
❖   Define and explain the concept of separate corporate personality.
❖   Refer to the decision in *Salomon v Salomon and Co Ltd* (1897) (House of Lords).
❖   Define and explain the concept of limited liability.
❖   Compare and contrast the issue of corporate liability with liability in a partnership.
❖   Evaluate and comment on the consequences of these two concepts for the development of company law.

ANSWER

A company is a legal abstraction or an artificial person that business people have found to be a highly convenient framework for carrying on a wide variety of commercial activities. There are many different kinds of companies, but the one thing they all have in common is that legally, once a company is registered, it has a separate legal identity or corporate personality. In other words, a company has a legal existence that is completely separate from the human beings who manage the company's affairs.

CORPORATE PERSONALITY

A company, being an artificial person, cannot physically do anything. Everything is carried out by human beings (the directors, officers and employees) in the name of the company. The law regards a company as a legal person with its own legal rights and obligations. It follows that if a wrong is done to a company it is the company, and not those who own the company's shares, that has the right to sue. Conversely, a person who is injured by a company will have the right to sue the company, but will not have the right to sue the company's shareholders or its officers.

This well-established principle that a company is a legal person in its own right was laid down by the House of Lords in *Salomon v Salomon and Co Ltd* (1897) and in particular, Lord Macnaghten's judgment. *Salomon* is regarded as one of the most important cases in English law, due to the legal protection that it offers to the shareholders and the officers of companies. Salomon was a sole trader who sold his business to his newly formed company. The company paid the purchase price partly by receiving a loan from Salomon, secured by all the company's assets. Unsecured creditors lent the new company more money, but the company was not profitable and was wound up. Secured creditors are entitled to be paid first out of the remaining assets of the company. This meant Salomon was entitled to be repaid his loan first. The unsecured creditors claimed that Salomon should pay their debts personally because he was the same person as the company. The House of Lords held that as a lawfully registered company, it had a separate legal identity from that of its only main shareholder, Salomon. Salomon's only obligation was to pay the price for his shares and not to repay the company's debts.

However, the fact that a company has a separate legal identity also has other consequences as set out in *Macaura v Northern Assurance Ltd* (1925) and *Tunstall v Steigmann* (1962).

Although a company is regarded as a legal person, it does not have human characteristics. A company does not enjoy human rights such as the right to vote at elections. A further consequence of corporate personality is that a company can be a taxpayer in its own right. This means that a company has to file a tax return and pay tax on its taxable income, entirely separately from the individuals who carry on its business. Similarly, the company owns its property and company property is not the property of the directors, the shareholders or anyone else. If the directors, officers and employees make a profit, it goes to the company as the company's income. If the company's board of directors passes a resolution to declare a dividend in order to return some of that profit to the shareholders, the dividend payments are the income of the shareholders and not of the company.

SHARES AND LIMITED LIABILITY

In *Salomon*, it was held that Mr Salomon was not personally liable for the debts of the company. When people buy shares in a limited company, the only commitment that they make is that they agree with the company that they will pay the price of the shares. Generally, these days, the full price is paid immediately, but this is not always the case.

If a company goes into liquidation, the shareholders will become liable to pay the amount outstanding on their shares to the company when payment becomes due under the terms of the contract that they made with the company. If the shares were transferred to another person before their full price had been paid to the company, the person taking the shares would have taken over liability to pay the rest of the price. None of the shareholders would have assumed liability to pay the debts of the company.

It must be emphasised that although a shareholder in a limited company will have limited liability, the company itself will not. If a company has debts it must pay them, even if this means selling all of its assets and going into liquidation.

Nonetheless, a company is founded on the concept of shares in the undertaking. A share in the company operates not only as a right to a proportion of the profits, if any, but also as a limitation of the shareholder's liability should the enterprise fail.

Contrast this with the position of a partner in a partnership – each of the partners is liable to outsiders for all of the partnership debts to the full extent of his or her personal fortune, whichever partner or partners caused the losses. A partner accepts unlimited liability for debts incurred by the partnership. It was this difference from simple partnership that led ultimately to one of the most important characteristics of the modern commercial company, a limit on the liability of the shareholders for the company's debts.

The idea therefore arose of a share in a company that can be freely traded at whatever price people are prepared to pay for it. In this way, a company's own trading activities can give rise incidentally to an entirely different trading activity, the buying and selling of its shares by people who may be otherwise unconnected with the company.

In summary, these twin ideas:

(1) limiting one's liability to pay for the losses of an enterprise
(2) without limiting the right to sell one's shares in the profits,

largely explain the universal adoption of the company framework for the conduct of all kinds of commercial activities during the last 150 years. The independent marketability of company shares in particular brought with it access to money raised from the general public (e.g. the London Stock Exchange), as opposed to having to seek out potential investors individually.

Common Pitfalls ✗

A lack of structure and a non-committal introduction/conclusion are undesirable in essay questions. This essay question specifically directs you to discuss the principles of separate corporate personality and limited liability. Ensure you narrow your discussion and deal with each of these topics fairly equally and in the same depth. Students should also be wary of writing an answer with 'too much opinion, and not enough law'.

Aim Higher ★

An essay question gives far more scope for students to express their own ideas than does a problem-type question. Students can perform very well in essay questions where the student has understood the subject and feels confident in it. The scope for achieving a very good mark in an essay is enhanced because of the flexibility that the essay-form of question offers. Here, think about the underlying policy implications of separate personality and limited liability which determine the limits of the current law.

QUESTION 39

Gina and Nigel wish to start up a business as mountaineering guides and instructors. Gina and Nigel have approached the bank for a loan to pay for the mountaineering equipment. The bank is willing to lend the money provided that Gina and Nigel decide on the business medium they are going to use and that they provide security for the loan. Nigel owns his own home but Gina rents a flat. Advise Gina and Nigel as to:

(a) their choice of a business medium and the advantages and disadvantages of same;
(b) the extent to which their liability for debts will be limited;
(c) the degree of management and control they will each be able to exercise in the business; and
(d) any public disclosure requirements.

Answer Plan

The focus of this question is to determine the most appropriate form of legal business structure for the mountaineering venture proposed by Gina and Nigel. Taking into consideration the facts concerning Gina and Nigel's business plans, analyse each of the following issues:

❖   the advantages of limited liability;

❖   the desire for the business to have control over membership;

❖   Gina and Nigel's involvement in management; and

❖   any public disclosure requirements.

ANSWER

Every small business initially needs to decide on the most appropriate legal form of business structure to carry out its enterprise. When two or more people go into business together, with the intention of making a profit for themselves, they must do so as a partnership, a limited liability partnership (LLP) or a company.

It is important for Gina and Nigel to be aware of the ways in which the relationship between partners of a general partnership differ from those of members of a limited company. These differences are important in determining the most suitable legal form to be selected for the carrying on of a business. Much will depend on the priorities, circumstances and risks of the entrepreneurs Gina and Nigel.

PROS AND CONS OF FORMING A PARTNERSHIP

Partnership is a contractual relationship and the partners (e.g. Gina and Nigel) enter into a contract with each other and agree the terms that will govern their business relationship. **Section 24** of the **Partnership Act 1890 (PA 1890)** sets out nine terms which are implied into the contract made by the partners. In addition, the Act sets out the three fiduciary duties which partners owe each other. If Gina and Nigel opt to form a partnership, they will both manage and be responsible for the business's debts and operations. Each partner contributes skills, money and time, and each shares in the company's profits and losses. The accounts of the partnership do not have to be publicly disclosed. The biggest advantage of a general partnership is the tax benefit. Businesses structured as partnerships do not pay income tax. Instead, all profits and losses are passed through to the individual partners. The partnership still files a tax return stating the business's profits and losses, but it does not pay taxes on the income. The partners must also file tax returns that show their individual shares of the company's profits and losses – although partners are not treated as employees.

The disadvantages of forming a general partnership are typically legal liability and management issues. First, partnership brings with it personal liability for all the business's obligations and debts. If the partnership is sued, all damages awarded are the responsibility of the individual partners. Further, most partnerships allow any partner to make decisions on behalf of the partnership. Even if a partner is acting on their own, all partners are responsible for the outcome of those decisions. Second, with respect to the degree of management control, all partners in a general partnership have a right to be involved in the management of the firm: **PA 1890, s 24(2)(a)**. For example, partners can make investments from their personal finances and the money invested is then owned by all partners, so it's easy for questions of reimbursement to arise. What if one partner didn't want the business to use that money and doesn't want the business to repay it? The same kinds of issues can arise with purchases for the business or even with decisions on which suppliers or clients to take on. If each partner has equal power and responsibility this can sometimes cause problems unless proper guidelines are set out. Partnerships are often formed among friends and colleagues, such as Gina and Nigel, which can make matters even more delicate.

PROS AND CONS OF FORMING A COMPANY

In recent years it has become increasingly easy to run a company due to the provisions of the **Companies Act 2006 (CA 2006)**. There are several key reasons why companies are so popular as a legal form of business in the United Kingdom; bear in mind that over 90 per cent of companies have five or fewer shareholders. The perceived advantages are prestige, legitimacy and the credibility that forming a company confers on the venture. However, the disadvantages of managing a company are regulatory requirements (to hold meetings, prepare and file accounts, etc.). On a positive note, there may also be considerable tax advantages from incorporation as a limited liability company as corporation tax is much lower than personal income tax.

In respect of liability, a limited liability company would offer distinct advantages to Gina and Nigel in the sense that, as members of a limited liability company, their liability would be limited to the extent of the capital contribution to the company as opposed to their being exposed to unlimited personal liability up to the full extent of their private wealth: *Salomon v Salomon & Co Ltd* (1897).

A problem Gina and Nigel face is that one or more of them (most likely Nigel, who owns his own home) will be required by the bank to stand as guarantor/surety for the debts of the company in order to operate with an overdraft from the bank. Effectively, Nigel's home is at risk if the company becomes unable to pay its debts, so limited liability in his case is illusory.

In a company, in contrast to a partnership, management is delegated to the board of directors. The problem is that, even if they are both made directors of their company initially, directors can be removed by ordinary resolution of the AGM with special notice under **CA 2006, s 168**. However, this could be avoided by drafting a clause in the new company's articles whereby, in the event of a resolution to remove a director from the board, the shares held by that director would give him or her two votes per share in a poll, so that a resolution to remove him or her could be defeated. This was established in *Bushell v Faith* (1970). In addition, in a small, quasi-partnership company such as this, an attempt to remove a member form the board would enable that person to petition on the grounds of unfair prejudice under **CA 2006, s 994**. This would enable the court to order that the shares of the petitioner be purchased by the company or by other shareholders at a valuation fixed by the court: **CA 2006, s 994**.

As regards the need for public disclosure of the affairs of a limited liability company, as long as the company could qualify as a 'small' company under the criteria fixed by the **CA 2006**, the extent of the disclosure of its affairs would be greatly reduced. The criteria are two out of three (tested every other year) of:

❖ Turnover – not more than £5.6m;
❖ Balance sheet total – not more than £2.8m;
❖ Number of employees – Not more than 50; **ss 382** and **383**.

The **Companies Act 2006** is an attempt to promote small business and to keep the regulatory burden to a minimum. The new Act is written in plain English and is more user-friendly than earlier versions, but it is still vast, with more than 1,300 sections. To this extent, the threat of disclosure is greatly diminished and the small company can enjoy almost the same degree of privacy in respect of its affairs as a partnership.

In conclusion, on balance and taking into account Gina's and Nigel's priorities, circumstances and risks, the advantages of incorporation outweigh the problems associated with it, including the cost involved in setting up the company. The pair should therefore be advised that, subject to having taken the right precautions fixing the constitution of the company, they would benefit from incorporation as a private limited liability company. Nevertheless, there remains a disconnection between the legal ideal of limited liability on the one hand and the economic reality that banks will continue to request personal guarantees from small companies, on the other.

> ## Common Pitfalls ✗
>
> Avoid spending too much time, if any, discussing another legal business structure, namely that of the sole trader. Running the mountaineering business as a sole tradership is simply not an option here as the business involves two people, Gina and Nigel.

> ## Aim Higher ★
>
> Aim to assist Gina and Nigel in making a decision about the most appropriate legal business structure for their mountaineering venture by clearly explaining the advantages and disadvantages of a partnership and a company. Think about the types of risk involved in such a business and the benefits of limited liability.

QUESTION 40

COMPANY LAW MULTIPLE CHOICE QUESTIONS

1. A business is registered under the name Nottingham Trading Limited. Which one of the following must the business be?

    a. A public limited company
    b. A partnership
    c. A private limited company
    d. Either a private limited company or a private unlimited company

2. Jessica owns 100 shares in a private limited company that has debts amounting to ten times its assets. The company is unable to pay the debts and creditors are threatening to petition to wind up the company. Jessica has paid half the nominal price of her shares. Which of the following statements is true?

    a. As the company is limited it need not pay its debts.
    b. Limited liability will mean that Jessica has to pay nothing towards the company's debts.
    c. The amount of the company's debts must be paid by all shareholders in proportion to their shareholding.
    d. Jessica must pay the other half of the nominal price of her shares. Beyond that, she need pay no more.

3. Which of the following is not a legal person?

   a. A small family company
   b. A Public Limited Company
   c. The BBC
   d. A small firm of chartered accountants

4. Which of the following resolutions may be used to increase a company's authorised capital?

   i.   Ordinary resolution
   ii. Written resolution
   iii. Special resolution

   a. (i) only
   b. (ii) only
   c. (iii) only
   d. Both (i) and (ii)
   e. Neither (i) nor (ii)
   f. Neither (ii) nor (iii)

5. Which of the following is correct?

   i. One is prohibited from registering a limited company with the same name as a company already on the register.
   ii. The name of every public company must end with the words 'public limited company' or the abbreviation 'plc'.

   a. (i) only
   b. (ii) only
   c. Both (i) and (ii)
   d. Neither (i) nor (ii)

6. Which one of the following statements is false?

   a. A public company must have at least two directors.
   b. A private company must have at least one director.
   c. Both public and private companies must have a qualified company secretary.

7. Incorporating a company has many advantages. Which of the following is in fact a disadvantage of incorporation?

   a. Pay tax at the corporate tax rate
   b. Resources needed from **Companies Act 2006** compliance
   c. Separate corporate identity
   d. Limited liability
   e. Contractual capacity

8. Consider the following:

   i.   The **Companies Act 2006** adopts a new 'think small' approach for private companies.
   ii. Table A articles of association are to be replaced with three new sets of model articles specifically for: (a) private limited companies; (b) public companies; and (c) companies limited by guarantee.
   iii. Private companies will no longer be required to have a company secretary.
   iv. Companies will no longer need to have an authorised share capital.
   v.   The residential addresses of directors will not be published by the Registrar of Companies.

   Which of the above statements is true?

   a. (i), (ii) and (iv) only
   b. (ii) and (iii) only
   c. (iii) and (iv) only
   d. All of the statements

9. Which one of the offences listed below can a company commit?

   a. Murder
   b. Treason
   c. Sexual offences
   d. Conspiracy to defraud
   e. Bigamy

10. A share is:

   a. a piece of personal property and a chose in action; OR
   b. a debt.

ANSWERS ---

1. c
2. d
3. d (it is most likely a partnership with no separate corporate personality)
4. a ((i) only)
5. c
6. c
7. b
8. d
9. d
10. a

Employment Law

INTRODUCTION

Employment law covers a multitude of legal issues. There is no one comprehensive code for employment law. The law relating to employment is derived from both common law and legislation. As the relationship between employer and employee is contractual, the general principles of contract law must constantly be taken into account as well.

Nevertheless, despite the extensive law that governs employment, it is a myth that employment laws mean an employer can never dismiss anyone. An employer can normally dismiss unsatisfactory employees as long as the dismissal is carried out fairly according to the **Employment Rights Act 1996**. If an employer dismisses an employee unfairly, the employee may be able to make a claim for compensation. This could end up as a risky, time-consuming and very expensive course of action.

When hiring employees, the law provides that an employer must not discriminate on the grounds of sex, race, disability, marital status or sexual orientation. The new **Equality Act 2010** consolidates the complicated and numerous array of Acts and Regulations which formed the basis of anti-discrimination law.

In general terms, apart from the employment contract, what can be expected from employees? Employees should be honest, obedient and not act against the employer's interests. In addition, they should be competent, and should work carefully and industriously. They should not disclose confidential information about the employer unless it is in the public interest, in which case the law protects 'whistleblower' employees: **Public Interest Disclosure Act 1998**. Employees have a duty to take reasonable care of the employer's property. Any patents, discoveries or inventions made during working hours will usually belong to the employer, unless the employment contract states otherwise or by agreement.

An employer has a duty to behave reasonably in terms of the employment, practise good industrial relations, provide a written statement of terms of employment, including disciplinary procedures and grievance procedures, and pay the minimum wage or more as agreed (men and women are to be paid equally for the same work). An employer must also take reasonable care to ensure the safety and health of its employees.

The most important advice for a business law student studying the employment law component of the course is to confirm precisely which aspects of employment law are to be covered in the syllabus. It is highly unlikely that the whole of the field of employment law can or will be covered in anything except a specialist employment law course.

QUESTION 41

You are the human resources manager of a large aviation company and you have been asked to give the firm's managers training in employment law. Explain on what grounds a dismissal from employment will be unfair.

Answer Plan

The student is asked to discuss dismissal from the employer's point of view. This means focusing on the lawful grounds set out in the **Employment Rights Act 1996 (ERA 1996)**, on which an employer may base a decision to dismiss.

- Introduce the **ERA 1996**.
- The employee must have one year's continuous service to be able to rely on statutory rights for unfair dismissal: s **94(1)** of the **ERA 1996**.
- Two-step analysis: (1) Has the employee been dismissed? (2) Was the dismissal carried out by the employer in a procedurally fair manner?
- Note the reasons for a 'fair' dismissal provided by s **98** of the **ERA 1996**.
- Discuss the nature of a 'procedurally fair' dismissal under s **98A** of the **ERA 1996**; *Post Office v Foley* (2000); and **Sched 2** to the **Employment Act 2002**.
- Note that the burden of proof lies with the employer to show that the dismissal was fair.

ANSWER

The human resources (HR) manager should begin his or her training session by introducing staff to the **Employment Rights Act 1996**. The **ERA 1996** sets out the law for when a dismissal will be fair and this is the aim of the bank: to ensure that any dismissals it undertakes are fair and will not lead to claims for unfair dismissal by an employee.

In particular, **s 94(1)** of the **ERA 1996** gives a statutory right to employees not to be unfairly dismissed if they have been continuously employed for at least one year. The key points to ensure staff understand are:

(1)   The dismissal will only be 'unfair' if the reason for the dismissal was outside one of the 'fair' reasons set out in **s 98** of the **ERA 1996**; and

(2)   The employer acted unreasonably in deciding to dismiss the employee.

Under **s 98** of the **ERA 1996**, the aviation company may lawfully terminate a contract of employment in several ways:

❖   Notice – one or other of the parties might give the required notice to terminate the contract (**s 86** of the **ERA 1996** sets out the minimum period of notice which the employer must give).

❖   Agreement – both parties might agree to end the contract. For example, the employee resigns giving the required notice.

❖   The employee might complete the task for which s/he is employed, or might work the whole of the time period specified in the contract.

❖   Frustration – the contract might become frustrated if it becomes impossible to perform or radically different from what the parties contemplated when they made the contract. The frustrating event must not be the fault of either of the parties. Long-term sickness might result in frustration of the contract: *Egg Stores (Stamford Hill) Ltd v Leibovici* (1977).

Section 98 of the **ERA 1996** also states that it is for the employer to show the reason(s) for the dismissal:

(a)   Relates to the capability or qualifications of the employee for performing work of the kind that s/he was employed by the employer to do (*Egg Stores*, *International Sports Co Ltd v Thomson* (1980));

(b)   Relates to the conduct of the employee (*Pepper v Webb* (1969), *Gardiner v Newport County Council* (1974));

(c)   The employee was made redundant (see **s 139(1)** of the **ERA 1996**);

(d)   The employee could not continue to work in the position that s/he held without contravention, either by him/her or his/her employer, of a duty or restriction imposed by or under statute (*Mathieson v Noble & Sons Ltd* (1972)); or

(e)   Some other substantial reason.

If an employee decides to bring a claim for unfair dismissal against the aviation company, the first step the employee must prove is that s/he has been dismissed in accordance with the terms of the **ERA 1996**. **Section 95** of the ERA provides a statutory definition of dismissal which states that an employee is dismissed if: (a) the employer terminates the contract, with or without notice; (b) a fixed-term contract expires; or (c) the employee is constructively dismissed.

If the aviation company can show that the dismissal was for one of the reasons in **s 98** of the **ERA 1996**, the next step is to decide whether the bank carried out the dismissal in a procedurally fair manner: **s 98A** of the **ERA 1996**. **Schedule 2** to the **Employment Act 2002** sets out a standard minimum procedure for a fair dismissal. This would involve:

(1) The company drafting a written statement of grounds for action to be provided to the employee and inviting the employee to meet to discuss the matter;
(2) The hearing meeting. After this, the company will inform the employee of its decision and notify him or her of the right to appeal against the decision;
(3) The appeal meeting, if required.

In deciding whether an employer's procedures for dismissal were fair, the employment tribunal will apply the 'band of reasonable responses' test to the facts. This is an objective test. The test is whether a reasonable employer could have acted in the same way as the employer (the company) who dismissed the employee. This test was affirmed by the Court of Appeal in the case of *Post Office v Foley* (2000).

Aviation company staff should also be made aware that the burden of proof is on the employer to show that the reason(s) for the dismissal falls within one of the matters listed and that the dismissal was procedurally fair.

In conclusion, if the employer is not able to prove these two elements, it will be judged that the employee was unfairly dismissed. Consequently, the unfairly dismissed employee will be entitled to three possible remedies: reinstatement, re-engagement or compensation.

Common Pitfalls ✘

Avoid undertaking a purely practical analysis of the facts with little or no reference to relevant statutory provisions or case law. Failure to support conclusions with legal analysis citing relevant case law and legislation will be marked down accordingly.

Aim Higher ★

Discuss the role of the Employment Tribunal which has jurisdiction to hear employment cases and appeals.

QUESTION 42

Babette has worked at the Ocean Club as a croupier (someone who presides at a gambling table) for the past eight years. The Ocean Club operates casinos all over England. Babette's weekly wage is £400 and she has no other income, savings or assets. On 1 October 2008, when she arrived at the Club for work, her line manager, Paul, told her that her services were no longer required and that she should go home. Paul explained that he had noticed recently that there had been a run of big wins on the roulette table on nights when she was working. He said that CCTV footage showed her acting furtively when she spun the roulette wheel and that he thought she was influencing where the ball came to rest so as to benefit punters with whom he suspected she was in league.

Babette vehemently denied the allegations and asked to see the offending CCTV footage, but Paul refused to show it to her, saying 'The camera never lies.' Babette became very agitated, swore at Paul and yelled at him, 'Stuff your job!'

On 3 October 2008, Babette received a letter from Paul saying that because she had been caught red-handed stealing from the Club and because of her unacceptable behaviour towards him when confronted with it, he had no choice but to terminate her contract with immediate effect, and that he would not be paying her any money in lieu of notice.

Advise Babette of her rights, if any, against the Ocean Club. Explain where her case will be heard and the procedure both immediately before and during the hearing as well as the remedies she will be entitled to, if successful.

Answer Plan

This is a demanding problem question, which requires the student to apply the relevant sections of the **Employment Rights Act 1996** and case law to a wrongful dismissal. The problem raises the issue of whether the summary (instant) dismissal was fair. In other words, in this problem the employee was dismissed on the spot without notice. Employers are permitted to summarily dismiss an employee, but only for specific reasons.

- ❖ Explain the nature of a summary dismissal under s 1 of the **Employment Rights Act 1996**.
- ❖ Note that the ground of dishonesty can found an instant dismissal.
- ❖ Consider whether Babette qualifies under the Act to make a statutory claim of unfair dismissal (does she have a minimum of one year's service?).

❖   Examine the facts to determine if Babette was fairly or unfairly dismissed
       in all the circumstances.
❖   Apply the 'reasonableness' test.
❖   Explain how Babette could enforce her claim and how she could fund the
       action to the employment tribunal.
❖   Briefly set out the procedure for making a claim against the employer.
❖   Consider remedies available to Babette if her claim is successful.

ANSWER

Babette has been summarily dismissed. She has been dismissed from her position as a
croupier by Paul, her line manager, who we presume has the required authority from
the employer, Ocean Club, to make this type of decision.

As she has been employed by the Ocean Club for eight years, which is far more than
one year's continuous employment required by **s 94(1)** of the **Employment Rights Act
1996 (ERA 1996)**, Babette can rely on her statutory right not to be unfairly dismissed. In
this case, Babette has a possible claim for wrongful dismissal against the Ocean Club,
because she has in fact been summarily dismissed, that is, dismissed without notice.
Babette does not believe that her conduct justifies a summary dismissal. However, the
Ocean Club is entitled to summarily dismiss Babette if her conduct is a sufficient
repudiation of the employment contract. There is case-law precedent, which is
authority for the Ocean Club to summarily dismiss Babette on the ground of
dishonesty: *Sinclair v Neighbour* (1967).

The time limit for Babette to bring an application for unfair dismissal is three months
from the effective date of termination of the employment; here, the termination took
effect on 1 October 2008, when Paul told her that her services were no longer required
and that she could go home: **s 97(b)** of the **ERA 1996**.

The onus is on Babette to show that she has been dismissed within the meaning of
s 95 of the **ERA 1996**. Here, there has been express termination by Paul, her line
manager, who has the authority to act on behalf of her employer, Ocean Club. The
onus then shifts to the Ocean Club to establish that the dismissal was fair and within
one of the reasons provided in **s 98** of the **ERA 1996**. In this case, the reason given by
the Ocean Club for summarily dismissing their employee Babette, relates to her
conduct. An employer must satisfy the reasonableness test. The factors used to
determine reasonableness are as follows:

(a) Length of service (in this case Babette has eight years' service);

(b) Previous disciplinary record (no evidence of any previous disciplinary matters against Babette in that time);

(c) Any mitigating circumstances, such as use of disciplinary procedures.

In relation to (c) above, no proper investigation was carried out by the line manager Paul or her employer. Further, Paul refused her request to see the CCTV footage. Failure to comply with a disciplinary procedure renders the dismissal automatically unfair.

In terms of enforcement, Babette's claim for wrongful dismissal must be made to an Employment Tribunal. Unfortunately, no Legal Aid is available, so Babette will have to represent herself, or pay for representation (or find a solicitor who will act on a no win, no fee basis). As Babette has little money, she should go to a Citizens Advice Bureau (CAB) or law centre where she will be means-tested. Before the hearing, the Advisory, Conciliation and Arbitration Service (ACAS) will get in touch with the parties to see if a settlement can be reached; if so, any settlement will be binding. If a settlement between Babette and the Ocean Club cannot be reached, there will be a hearing before the Employment Tribunal.

The Employment Tribunal consists of a panel of three persons, including the chair (a lawyer of at least seven years' standing) and two lay members (one from a trade union and one from management). At the Employment Tribunal, the procedure for case presentation is a fairly informal procedure as often the litigants represent themselves.

If Babette's claim for wrongful dismissal is successful, her remedies will include either reinstatement or re-engagement (**s 113** of the **ERA 1996**) or financial compensation (**s 119** of the **ERA 1996**). **Section 86** of the **ERA 1996** sets out the minimum amount of notice that the Ocean Club should have paid Babette, which would amount to one week's pay for every year of service. As Babette has eight years' service she would be entitled to at least £3,200 for loss of wages and possibly for the loss of other benefits such as life and health insurance: *Shove v Downs Surgical plc* (1984).

Common Pitfalls ✗

Avoid treating a problem question as an invitation to write an abstract essay about the employment issues involved in the problem. Avoid writing out verbatim sections of the legislation; it is recommended you merely refer to the relevant section number. The facts are all-important and application of the relevant legislation and case law to the facts is essential. Do not assume facts which are not given.

> ### Aim Higher ★
>
> Consider the order in which you wish to deal with the issues raised by
> the facts and bear in mind the need to present points in a coherent
> and logical way. Identify:
>
> ❖   any detailed factors that an employment tribunal may take into
>   account; and
> ❖   any details of the facts that will assist.

QUESTION 43

Critically analyse the new **Equality Act 2010** in relation to disability discrimination
at work.

> ### Answer plan
>
> This essay question invites the student to explain the provisions of the **Equality Act
> 2010**. Disabled people are a group of people who, in their capacity as employees or
> workers, have particular rights at work.

ANSWER

Disabled workers share the same general employment rights as other workers.
However, there are also some special rights for disabled people under the new
Equality Act 2010. For example, when hiring employees, the law provides that an
employer must not discriminate on the grounds of sex, race, disability, marital status
or sexual orientation. The **Equality Act 2010** consolidates the complicated and
numerous array of Acts and Regulations that previously formed the basis of
anti-discrimination law. This consisted, primarily, of the **Equal Pay Act 1970**, the **Sex
Discrimination Act 1975**, the **Race Relations Act 1976**, the **Disability Discrimination Act
1995** and three major statutory instruments protecting against discrimination in
employment on the grounds of religion or belief, sexual orientation and age.

The new **Equality Act 2010** shares the same goals as the four major EU Equal
Treatment Directives, whose provisions it mirrors and implements. The Act requires
equal treatment in access to employment as well as private and public services,
regardless of the protected characteristics of age, disability, gender reassignment,
marriage and civil partnership, race, religion or belief, sex, and sexual orientation. In

the case of gender, there are special protections for pregnant women. However, the Act allows transsexual people to be barred from gender-specific services if that is 'a proportionate means of achieving a legitimate aim'. In the case of disability, employers and service providers are under a duty to make reasonable adjustments to their workplaces to overcome barriers experienced by disabled people. In this regard, the Equality Act 2010 did not change the previous law.

EMPLOYERS AND THE EQUALITY ACT 2010

Under the Equality Act 2010, it is unlawful for employers to discriminate against disabled people. The disability parts of the Act cover:

❖ application forms;
❖ interview arrangements;
❖ aptitude or proficiency tests;
❖ job offers;
❖ terms of employment including pay;
❖ promotion, transfer and training opportunities;
❖ work-related benefits such as access to recreation or refreshment facilities;
❖ dismissal or redundancy;
❖ discipline and grievances.

An employer must also make reasonable changes to applications, interviews and work so that a disabled person is not disadvantaged. These are known as 'reasonable adjustments'. In addition, the Act limits when a person recruiting for work may make enquiries about a job applicant's health or disability.

Under the Equality Act 2010, an employer must not treat a disabled person less favourably because the person has a disability – this is known as 'direct discrimination'. Neither is indirectly discriminating against a disabled person, unless there is a fair and balanced reason for same, permitted. Furthermore, it is unlawful to directly discriminate against or harass a person because they are associated with a disabled person or the person is wrongly thought to be disabled.

Victimisation on the grounds of disability is also an important issue. Under the Act, it is unlawful to victimise anyone. Victimisation might arise because the person has taken, or is believed likely to take, action under the Act. Examples of victimisation include making a complaint or taking a case to a tribunal or court. Or it might be because they have helped somebody to make a complaint or to take other action.

Finally, an employer cannot select an employee for redundancy just because s/he is disabled. The criteria used to select people for redundancy must not put disabled people at a disadvantage, unless there is a fair and balanced reason. The employer must make reasonable adjustments to any criteria used to select employees for redundancies. For example, it could be a reasonable adjustment for the employer to discount disability-related sickness absence when using attendance as one basis for selection.

It is essential to observe that the rights outlined above do not just apply in an employment context. The **Equality Act 2010** also covers other forms of work like partnerships, contract work, or holding an office such as a director of a business.

In conclusion, while the new Act does not make any great strides in changing the previous law relating to discrimination on the grounds of disability, it has consolidated much of the key employment law into one major source. This has provided an opportunity to consider how it can best be recast for the benefit of those who will use it.

Common Pitfalls ✗

An essay should not be an encyclopaedia of the irrelevant, no matter how learned, but a focused answer to a specific question – do not simply recite your lecture notes or a chapter from a book.

Aim Higher ★

The main aim in writing an essay answer is to adhere as closely as possible to the question asked. It is difficult to get the balance right between comprehensive coverage of the range of points that can be made, and sufficient depth in the treatment of each. A good approach is to explain the key employment rights and illustrate them with practical examples that the new Act is designed to deal with. Make express reference to the essay title every now and then, and be sure to finish the essay with a conclusion that ties together your thoughts and refers back to the essay question.

QUESTION 44

Your employer, a bank, is under considerable financial strain as a result of the recent international credit crunch and subprime mortgage debacle. The board of directors has been considering all manner of cost-cutting measures. The board has requested you to prepare a paper for the next board meeting on the subject of the proposed redundancy programme, involving approximately 95 employees, and precisely how this would be lawfully achieved.

Answer Plan

This question requires the student to explain the law related to large-scale redundancies and collective consultation.

- ❖ Define 'redundancy' under s 139(1) of the **Employment Rights Act 1996**.
- ❖ In order to claim redundancy, an employee must have at least two years' continuous employment since reaching the age of 18.
- ❖ Note **Part IV** of the **Trade Union and Labour Relations (Consolidation) Act 1992** and **Information and Consultation of Employees Regulations 2004**.
- ❖ Explain how the collective consultation procedure works and the need to notify the Department for Business, Enterprise and Regulatory Reform (BERR).
- ❖ Discuss the selection criteria and offers of suitable alternative employment: *Williams v Compair Maxam Ltd* (1982).
- ❖ Explain the consequences if the collective consultation is not carried out.

ANSWER

Redundancy is a form of dismissal from employment. According to **s 13(1)** of the **Employment Rights Act 1996**, valid reasons for employers to make their employees redundant include:

- ❖ The business is closing down or moving.
- ❖ New technology or a new system has made the job unnecessary.
- ❖ The job the employee was hired for no longer exists.
- ❖ The employer needs to cut costs and so staff numbers must be reduced.

In the bank's case, the last of these is a valid reason to contemplate a redundancy programme. The relevant legislation governing redundancies is also contained in **Part IV** of the **Trade Union and Labour Relations (Consolidation) Act 1992 (TULR(C)A 1992)** under the **Information and Consultation of Employees Regulations 2004**.

First, the board will need to be aware of the consultation procedure. The length of time required in connection with the consultation procedure is determined by the number of employees to be made redundant. The law provides that if at one establishment within a 90-day period there are fewer than 20 employees being made redundant, then the statutory minimum dismissal procedure should be followed. If there are 20 or more, then the collective consultation procedure applies instead. Here, the bank will have to initiate a collective consultation procedure as it contemplates a redundancy programme involving 95 employees. The bank must begin the consultation process at least 90 days before the first of the dismissals is to take effect (i.e. when the employment contract is terminated) as it is dealing with a group of 95 employees. The aim of collective consultation is to determine whether there is any suitable alternative employment for each individual in the group of 95 employees.

In summary, if the bank proposes to make collective redundancies it is required to consult in advance with representatives of the affected employees, and to notify the projected redundancies to the Department for Business, Enterprise and Regulatory Reform. The consultation must be completed before any notices of dismissal are issued to employees. If the bank fails to consult as required by the law, the employees may bring a complaint of failure to consult to an Employment Tribunal within three months of the last dismissals and unfair dismissal. If the tribunal upholds the complaint, the tribunal may make a protective award to the employees of up to 90 days' pay.

It will also need to be clarified to the board that, in order to select the 95 employees for the proposed redundancy programme, it is vital that the selection criteria should not be exclusively on the basis of 'last in first out'. In other words, the last 95 employees to be hired by the bank should not automatically comprise the group to be made redundant. Rather, the bank must, in addition to length of service, consider several issues in connection with each individual it is considering making redundant, namely:

- ❖ employee attendance/absence records;
- ❖ annual appraisals; and
- ❖ the bank's requirements.

The bank may attach different weight to each of the above issues, but then this should be fairly applied to each employee who is assessed for the redundancy programme: *Williams v Compare Maxam Ltd* (1982).

In terms of which employees are eligible for redundancy payments, eligibility is restricted to those employees with a minimum of two years' continuous service and then the amount of the payment is based on age. The bank will need to calculate the amount of the redundancy payment for each employee individually. The closer the employee is to retirement, the greater the cost to the bank of the redundancy payment:

(1) 18–21 years: half a week's pay for each completed year of service;
(2) 22–40 years: one week's pay for each completed year of service;
(3) 41 to normal retirement age (this may vary for some men and women): one-and-a-half weeks' pay for each completed year of service.

Twenty-one years is the maximum period of service that the bank will have to take into account.

If it is possible to redeploy staff in order to reduce operating costs, this would save future costs involved in recruiting new staff, so it is in the bank's commercial interest to do so, apart from any legal requirement.

On the other hand, if an employee is offered a new role within the bank, which is reasonable, and the employee nevertheless unreasonably rejects the bank's offer, then the employee cannot claim to have been made redundant and will lose the right to any redundancy payment. The case of *Taylor v Kent County Council* (1969) illustrates what was considered to be unsuitable alternative employment. In this case, the Council made Taylor, a middle-aged, long-standing school headmaster, redundant when his school merged with another school. The Council offered Taylor alternative employment at his headmaster salary, but only as a supply teacher. The court held that this form of alternative employment was not suitable, nor reasonable. Taylor had been made redundant and could claim a redundancy payment from the Council.

Common Pitfalls ✗

Avoid introductions that are so general that they could have been written in answer to ANY problem considering principles of employment law. Such introductions do not answer the question set; they are unrelated to the specific issue raised. Ensure that your introductory paragraph refers to the key issue raised by the problem.

Aim Higher ★

Conclude by summarising the outcomes for the party you were asked to advise – but only do this where you have not already given this type of conclusion at the end of the application for each issue, or where you want to conclude with a statement of the wider picture (i.e. all the issues taken together).

QUESTION 45

The downturn in the economy has had a severe impact on the aviation industry, resulting in a drop in demand for airline seats and cargo transport. Several of Zulu Aviation Ltd's routes are no longer making a profit. Zulu Aviation Ltd decides to cancel its Nottingham to Amsterdam and Zurich passenger routes. Mark, who has worked as an Airbus passenger pilot based in Nottingham for the past three years, is offered another job as a cargo pilot operating out of Scunthorpe, 75 miles away. Mark declines the job as he is not happy to move to Scunthorpe and regards the position as a demotion as he would earn less money as a cargo pilot.

▶ Advise Mark as to any possible claim that he could make against Zulu Aviation Ltd and whether his claim would be likely to succeed. Refer to relevant legislation and case law to support your answer.

Answer Plan

❖ Consider the difference between the statutory unfair dismissal and wrongful dismissal and why statutory unfair dismissal is the preferred remedy;

❖ Demonstrate knowledge of the lawful grounds for dismissal;

❖ Analyse whether the grounds for dismissing Mark were fair;

❖ Apply the relevant case law on redundancy grounds: *O'Brien v Associated Fire Alarms* (1968) and *Fuller v Stephanie Bowman* (1977) to Mark's situation.

ANSWER

As Mark's contract of employment has been terminated he is concerned to know whether he has a remedy for dismissal from his employment. Generally, a dismissed employee would prefer to sue for the statutory remedy of unfair dismissal rather than for wrongful dismissal. **Section 98** of the **Employment Rights Act 1996 (ERA 1996)** states that in determining whether or not the dismissal of an employee is fair or unfair, it is for the employer to show the reason for the dismissal. The five matters that can justify a dismissal include **s 98(2)(c)**: the reason for the dismissal was redundancy. In other words, a person who is made redundant is not regarded in law as having been unfairly dismissed.

In this case, we need to establish whether the ground for Mark's dismissal on the ground of redundancy is fair. If it is fair, then Mark could make a claim for a redundancy payment under **s 135** of **ERA 1996**. In order to do so, Mark will have to show that he has been:

1. *dismissed* and the reason for the dismissal was redundancy (**s 139 ERA 1996**); and
2. *employed continuously* by Gunnell Aviation for two years prior to dismissal (**s 155 ERA 1996**).

It seems clear that Mark has been dismissed and that the reason for his dismissal was redundancy as Zulu Aviation are ceasing to carry on certain business from Nottingham for the purposes of which Mark was employed. Cessation of business is one of the most common redundancy situations. So the remaining question to consider is whether his refusal to accept the job in Scunthorpe was reasonable or not (**s 138 ERA 1996**).

Is Mark's refusal of an offer of a different job in a nearby town reasonable? Applying the decision in *O'Brien v Associated Fire Alarms* (1969), in which there was no 'geographical mobility clause' in the contract, refusing an offer of a different job in a nearby town is reasonable. As a result, this causes redundancy. However, if Mark's employment contract with Zulu Aviation does include a mobility clause, the situation will be less clear.

However, refusing an offer of suitable alternative employment may be unreasonable according to *Fuller v Stephanie Bowman (Sales Ltd)* (1977) and so may prevent a successful claim for redundancy. In Mark's case, his refusal to accept the alternative job in Scunthorpe, 75 miles away, appears reasonable and his claim for redundancy payment would thus succeed.

One other issue to consider is whether the means by which Mark was selected for redundancy was unfair. If so, he may also be able to claim for unfair dismissal (**s 98 ERA**). However, in this case, there are no facts to suggest that Mark was unfairly dismissed as it is employees in Nottingham who are affected and he is in this group.

Common Pitfalls ✗

Avoid writing a purely practical analysis of the facts with little or no reference to relevant statutory provisions or case law. Failure to discuss the relevant legislation and case law will result in an answer containing 'all facts and no law' and will be marked down accordingly.

Aim Higher ★

This question calls for both effective deployment of the relevant legislation AND case law and an application of BOTH sources of law to the facts.

Intellectual Property Law

12

INTRODUCTION

Intellectual property law concerns the various rights that protect creative endeavour and innovation. Importantly, intellectual property rights (IPR) also protect the application of ideas and information that are of commercial value.

In a business law course, the intellectual property law syllabus will usually be limited to patents, copyright, moral rights, design, trade marks, passing off, geographical indications and breach of confidence.

Intellectual property law draws on other legal fields such as contract, tort, land, common law and equity. This means that it is sometimes regarded as a more difficult subject area. Nevertheless, as intellectual property law is also one of the most modern, cutting-edge law subjects, business law students tend to embrace it as they can immediately see its importance within the context of a knowledge-based economy.

Over the centuries, various rulers of the UK and its governments have recognised that protecting creative endeavour is crucial to the promotion of innovation and entrepreneurship. A legal framework has been created by various Acts of Parliament to provide creators/inventors with exclusive rights or a monopoly.

The key intellectual property rights for business law students are:

❖ 'Patents' – A patent is a statutory property right governed by the **Patents Act 1977**, which gives the patent owner the exclusive right to use certain inventions for up to 20 years.
❖ 'Copyright' – Copyright is a statutory right governed by the **Copyright, Designs and Patents Act (CDPA) 1988**, subsisting in original literary, dramatic, musical and artistic works, sound recordings, films, broadcasts, cable programmes and the typography of published editions. Copyright owners have several economic rights in their works, including the right to prevent unauthorised copyright and adaptations.

❖ 'Moral rights' – Moral rights are statutory rights under the **CDPA 1988**, which authors retain in their works, regardless of who owns the economic rights to the work.

❖ 'Trade marks' – Registered trade marks are statutory rights, as provided by the **Trade Marks Act 1994**. This gives the owner the exclusive right to use a distinctive sign (for example a name, symbol, tune, etc.) in relation to a product or service.

❖ 'Geographical indications' (or indications of source or appellations of origin) – These are signs assuring consumers that produce comes from, or has been processed in, a particular region renowned for the quality of such produce. Familiar examples include Champagne, Scotch whisky, Melton Mowbray pork pies and Parma ham. The UK is bound by **article 22(2)** of the international **Trade Related Aspects of Intellectual Property (TRIPS) Agreement** to prevent the use of any means in the designation or presentation of a good that indicates or suggests that the good in question originates in a geographical area, other than the true place of origin, in a manner that misleads the public as to the geographical origin of the good.

❖ 'Design' – A registered design is a statutory right under the **Registered Designs Act 1949**, which gives the exclusive right to use certain features of the appearance of a range of products. The unregistered design right is the right under the **CDPA 1988** to prevent copying of aspects of shape or configuration of an article.

The common law and equity also continue to feature in the protection of intellectual property as follows:

❖ 'Passing off' – Goodwill is a form of intangible property consisting of the market's perception of the quality and value of a business and its products, which can be protected by the common-law tort of passing off. Passing off is a common-law tort or cause of action used to prevent a third party from making misrepresentations that damage the goodwill of another.

❖ 'Breach of confidence' – The equitable doctrine of breach of confidence is used to protect certain confidential information which does not fall within the scope of the other intellectual property law systems set out above, against unauthorised disclosure or use.

Some intellectual property rights come into existence automatically (for example, copyright and the design right), while others take effect only upon completion of registration (patents, registered trade marks and registered designs).

Intellectual property protection also occurs at an international level and the above forms of intellectual property are included in the **TRIPS Agreement**, which was finalised at the end of the Uruguay Round of world trade negotiations in 1993.

A central theme running through the entire field of intellectual property law is the need to strike a balance between the interest of rights owners and the public. This is to ensure that innovations and creative endeavours are disseminated for the benefit of society as a whole.

QUESTION 46

An employee of Toflen Ltd has developed a revolutionary new chemical formula ('tetrafluorethylene'), which when applied to kitchen utensils prevents food from sticking. The company intends marketing the kitchen utensils coated with tetrafluorethylene under a commercial name attractive to potential customers. Tetrafluorethylene is not an easy name for consumers to remember, let alone pronounce. 'Teflon' is the name chosen by the marketing director as a play on words based on the company name. A product range logo will also be designed once the name is chosen. The company also wishes to enhance the sale of its utensils by giving them a more appealing, sleek, modern new shape. The in-house product testing and safety team are completing a detailed instruction sheet for consumers. Graphic designers are creating the product's packaging and have engaged a freelance artist to create some preliminary images. The marketing director is liaising with an advertising agency to create a catchy 30-second jingle to accompany the TV advertisement. A website for the product range is also in development.

Explain to Toflen Ltd the various areas of intellectual property law they need to consider protecting in advance of the product launch.

Answer plan

The aim of this problem question is to identify the range of intellectual property rights arising in the product.

❖ The company may be able to apply for patent protection of the chemical formula under the **Patents Act 1977**.

❖ The product mark and logo may be protected as registered trade marks under the **Trade Marks Act 1994**.

❖ The new design (shape and contours) may be eligible for registration under the **Registered Designs Act 1949**.

❖ The instruction sheet (literary work) and packaging (artistic work) may be automatically protected by the **Copyright, Designs and Patents Act 1988**. The advertising jingle will give rise to a variety of copyright works. The web content will also attract copyright protection for its content.

ANSWER

Several intangible intellectual property rights arise in connection with Toflen Ltd's new kitchen utensil product. Each element of the product will be analysed in turn.

PATENT RIGHTS

First, the new chemical formula 'tetrafluorethylene' gives rise to potential patent rights. The requirements for patents to be granted are governed by the **Patents Act (PA) 1977**. Patents can be applied for only in respect of inventions that are: new; involve an inventive step; are capable of industrial application; and do not relate to excluded subject matter (**s 1(1)** of the **PA 1977**). The purpose of patent rights is to encourage innovation by granting monopoly rights while at the same time making access to technological advances publicly available on expiry of the monopoly rights. However, **s 39(1)** of the Act states that an invention made by an employee shall be taken as belonging to his/her employer if the invention arose in the normal course of his/her duties. A granted patent has a duration of 20 years from the date of filing the application. If Toflen Ltd obtains a granted patent, it will have the sole monopoly right to exploit the chemical coating.

TRADE MARK RIGHTS

Teflon is probably a mark already used by another company and may not be available for registration and indeed may pose an infringement risk for Toflen Ltd.

It may be advisable for the company to rethink its product name or consider using the name 'Toflen'. If 'Toflen' is suitable, the company could apply to register it as a trade mark. According to **s 1(1)** of the **Trade Marks Act 1994**, a trade mark means 'any sign capable of being represented graphically which is capable of distinguishing goods or services of one undertaking from those of another undertaking'. As a matter of good practice, the company should conduct a preliminary trade mark search to ensure the mark 'Toflen' does not belong to anyone else. If this infringement search is clear, the company should ensure that the mark is capable of successful registration and will not be refused. The effect of a registered mark is to give the company exclusive rights in the UK for as long as the company uses the mark in commerce and continues to pay the required registration renewal fees. The company should use the symbol TM until the mark is registered and thereafter #rM to notify others of its trade mark rights in 'Toflen'. In respect of the Toflen logo, this would also be capable of registration as a trade mark.

DESIGN

In relation to the new, modern, sleek shape of the utensils, the company has two options to protect its design. First, the company could apply to register the utensil design under the **Registered Designs Act (RDA) 1949**. Under the Act, a design means the appearance of the whole or part of a product resulting from the features of, in particular, the lines, contours, colours, shapes, textures or materials of the product itself or its ornamentation. The design must be one that is applied to an article and must be novel in the sense of being new (**s 1(2)** of the **RDA 1949**). A registered design subsists for a maximum of 25 years. Alternatively, the company can rely on the lesser protection of the 'unregistered' design right, created under **s 213(2)** of the **Copyright, Designs and Patents Act (CDPA) 1988**. An unregistered design will subsist for a maximum of 15 years.

COPYRIGHT

The detailed product instruction sheet would attract copyright protection as an original literary work under **s 1(1) CDPA**. Copyright protects the way in which ideas are expressed, rather than the ideas themselves. A literary work does not have to be a work of literature. It has been held by the courts to include an instruction sheet. Copyright exists for different lengths of time, depending on the type of work concerned. Copyright in a literary work expires at the end of 70 years from the end of the calendar year in which the author dies. In the UK there is no requirement to formally register copyright. It can be useful to give notice of copyright by using the phrase '© Toflen Ltd 2008' on the sheet. In this case Toflen Ltd would own the copyright in the instruction sheet.

The product packaging could give rise to both copyright as an artistic work for the artwork and possibly design rights, depending on the nature of the packaging. The 30-second jingle gives rise to copyright as a musical work for the tune, copyright as a literary work for the lyrics, and copyright for the sound recording as well as copyright in the film of the TV advertisement. In relation to the product range website, copyright will arise in the web content and it is important to register the domain name to align with the product's trade mark name 'Toflen'.

In conclusion, it is clear that many forms of intellectual property rights need to be considered prior to the product launch. Intellectual property rights are also limited by jurisdiction and the company will need to consider whether it needs to register its intellectual property rights in any other countries in which it intends to market the utensils.

Common Pitfalls ✗

Methodically examine each element of the product. Each line of the problem question gives rise to important facts that need to be analysed in terms of which form of intellectual property protection is important.

QUESTION 47

Critically discuss the key advantages and disadvantages of patenting an invention under the **Patents Act 1977**.

Answer Plan

❖   Compile a list of advantages and discuss them in a logical order.
❖   Similarly, compile a list of disadvantages and discuss them in a logical order.
❖   Provide thoughtful concluding remarks based on the above analysis.

ANSWER

Patents protect new, industrially applicable inventions and give the inventor or proprietor (the 'patentee') a legally recognised monopoly to work the invention for a period of up to 20 years. There are both advantages and disadvantages to patent protection, as the procedure for obtaining a granted patent is costly, lengthy and complex. It is important to consider the pros and cons before either publishing the invention or applying for the patent.

ADVANTAGES OF PATENT PROTECTION

The key advantage of filing a patent is that a patent monopoly is granted for a firm duration of 20 years and can prevent unauthorised third parties from using the invention during that period. While under monopoly protection, the **Patent Act 1977** provides that only the patentee is lawfully allowed to commercially exploit the invention through manufacturing and licensing. The scope of that right in any particular case is determined by the claims in the patent specification. This usually includes reverse-engineering, since a valid patent protects the ideas and information in the way described in the patent's claims, and using such information obtained via reverse-engineering in the ways described in the patent claims will infringe the patent.

The patentee is even protected against someone who subsequently creates the same invention entirely through his or her own efforts.

Other advantages of obtaining a granted patent include the fact that the patentee has the ability to file for protection in other jurisdictions using the original priority date. Once the patent application is filed, the information contained in it can be freely disclosed without loss of proprietary rights.

In addition, the boundaries of subject matter susceptible to patent protection has expanded so that protection is available for certain inventions where that opportunity did not exist in the past. Together with novelty, inventive step or non-obviousness, and utility, the question of whether a particular subject matter is patentable is one of the fundamental requirements for patentability. This means that the system is flexible and capable of adapting.

Perhaps the most important advantage is that a patent is a form of property that can be licensed to generate royalties and future income. Once granted, the patent owner can sue for patent infringement dating back to the priority date. Nevertheless, there is no legal requirement to file for a patent and an inventor could decide to keep the invention secret, so the system is not mandatory. The decision to file a patent application is not irrevocable; it may be withdrawn at any time before publication by the Patent Office.

DISADVANTAGES OF PATENTING

On the other hand, the key disadvantage of filing a patent is that the patentee, in return for patent protection, must consent to publication of the details of the new invention. This means that third parties can 'invent around' or improve on the invention. Other significant disadvantages relate to the costs and length of time to secure a patent which, on average, takes over three years.

Some are disappointed by the fact that a patent provides a mere 20-year monopoly, after which anyone may exploit the invention. Furthermore, patent protection is territorial and will only cover the UK, although patents may, if certain requirements are met, be filed in other countries for an additional cost via the **European Patent Convention (EPC)** and **Patent Cooperation Treaty (PCT)** routes. The patent application may need to be translated if filed in other jurisdictions, further adding to the costs involved. If the **EPC** or **PCT** route is used, the patent application will still need to undergo a national phase in each designated country. As yet there is no single global patent in existence although the World Intellectual Property Organization (WIPO) is currently engaging in this debate. Many stakeholders in the patent system are calling for the creation of a global patent system to make it easier and faster for corporations to enforce their intellectual property rights around the world

Another disadvantage is the cost of obtaining a patent. Given the importance of the claims determining the scope of the patent monopoly, it is generally recommended that a patent specification be prepared by a patent attorney or a person familiar with the state of the art of the invention and the patent process. This increases the cost of the patent process.

Other important disadvantages of the patent system from the point of view of the patentee are that disclosures by others can ruin novelty. Nothing can be done if someone else engaged in similar research makes the invention public before a patentee applies for a patent. Even once the patent has been granted, opposition proceedings may be started. This means that the patent can be challenged and possibly revoked. Again on the subject of costs, the patentee must pay ever higher fees to continue to renew the patent until the 20-year monopoly has expired.

Although not required for legal protection, the patented invention should be marked with the granted patent number as a deterrent for potential infringers. Finally, unless the patent owner reserves its rights, once a patent product has been sold, the purchaser has an implied right to sell that product to anyone in the world, who in turn has the same right. This can cause problems for patentees who want to control commercial export and import of their products.

In conclusion, while there are certainly several disadvantages to the patent law system, the UK Patent Office reports steadily increasing levels of patent application activity. Indeed, patent activity is mushrooming across virtually every sector of the UK economy as patentees seek to gain a proprietary market advantage, an exclusive hold over a new technology. Registered patent rights have also seen a boom in revenues derived from patent licensing and have served as a hidden motive behind a number of the biggest corporate mergers in the last decade. It is not just the UK economy that is affected by these trends; patent activity is on the rise worldwide, spurred in part by the World Trade Organization's **Agreement on Trade-Related Aspects of Intellectual Property Rights (TRIPS)**. Concerns have been raised about the recent trends in patent activity – the patenting of biotechnological inventions, business methods and databases – and that these may actually stifle academic freedom, scientific inquiry and technological innovation. However, there is little doubt, as evidenced by dozens of studies by economists and Gower's *Review of Intellectual Property*, published in December 2006, that the patent system is, on balance, an effective instrument for fostering innovation and technology diffusion.

Common Pitfalls ✗

Never start an essay with the phrase, 'In this essay I am going to . . .'. The marker knows what you need to do. The sooner your writing focuses on the question, the more marks you will attract. One of the most common and useful beginnings to a patent law essay is to start with an explanation of what a patent does.

Aim Higher ★

This question encourages the student to carry out an objective evaluation of the advantages and disadvantages of patenting, drawing on all aspects of the patent law system, but using only relevant material. A critical essay requires strong discussion coupled with a sharp structure. Each argument should be supported with sufficient evidence, relevant to the point. You could comment on the practical and commercial difficulties faced by prospective patentees.

QUESTION 48

Buffy Bouffant, a hairdresser who owns her own salon, is a hair accessories designer and inventor in her spare time. She consults you regarding her latest invention, a new type of hair-straightening iron using super-smooth therma glass, which is an improvement on ceramic hair straighteners.

Buffy sold her rights to a previous hair product invention to an international company for a flat fee of £20,000, but feels she did not get as much as she could have for it because she sold after only having produced a working prototype. The purchaser has since gone on to sell millions and has made substantial profits from Buffy's earlier invention.

This time around, Buffy, who feels she has established her reputation as an inventor in the field, wishes to apply for a patent in the hope of achieving a better fee for her invention by offering it to several companies to bid on. Advise Buffy as to:

(1) The advantages and/or disadvantages of obtaining a patent;
(2) The patentability of her therma-glass hair straightener;

(3) The steps involved in the patenting process and any other relevant matters that she will need to consider.

Answer plan

This is a very practical problem requiring the student to be broadly familiar with the key aspects of the UK's patent law system.

❖ Consider the patentability of the therma-glass aspect of the hair straightener (a mechanical device) and confirm whether the four conditions for filing a patent set out in s 1(1) of the **Patents Act 1977** are met.

❖ Apply the concept of absolute novelty and the need for confidentiality prior to patent application.

❖ Set out the procedural process required to file a patent application.

ANSWER

Buffy can apply for a UK patent through the UK Intellectual Property Office to protect her new therma-glass hair straightener product if certain legal requirements are met. Under the **Patents Act 1977 (PA 1977)**, there is no definition of an invention. However, Buffy's patent application must comply with certain administrative formalities as well as meeting the requirements for a patentable invention. There are four key legal requirements that must be satisfied in order to conclude that a patentable invention exists in the new therma-glass hair straightener, so that Buffy should be granted a UK patent. The invention must:

(1) Be novel: **s 2** of the **PA 1977**;

(2) Involve an inventive step: **s 3** of the **PA 1977**. In other words, the invention must be a technical advance over existing technology ('the state of the art'), which is not obvious;

(3) Be capable of industrial application: **s 4** of the **PA 1977**;

(4) Not be excluded by law from being patented: **s 1(3)** of the **PA 1977** (e.g. not contrary to public policy or morality).

In relation to the novelty requirement, Buffy must ensure that she keeps the new therma-glass hair-straightener invention absolutely confidential until she files a patent application, otherwise the novelty of her invention will be destroyed. Once a patent application has been filed, Buffy will be able to freely disclose her invention to potential purchasers to bid on (unless the bidders agree to sign strongly drafted confidentiality/nondisclosure agreements).

We are told that Buffy's invention is an improvement on existing technology, so it is likely that the inventive step requirement will be met. Further, the industrial application of the invention should not be problematic as the product can be manufactured easily. Finally, there are no issues arising in relation to the invention being contrary to public policy or morality.

Therefore, assuming that Buffy's invention meets the four legal requirements for patentability, she should feel confident about filing her application with the UK Intellectual Property Office. The procedural steps will involve the following:

(1) Completing Patent Form 1/77. The patent application must comprise a specification containing a description of the invention, as well as a claim for the patent and any drawing referred to in the description of the claim as well as an abstract;

(2) Filing (**s 5(1)** of the **PA 1977**);

(3) Preliminary examination and limited search (**s 17** of the **PA 1977**) within 12 months from the filing date. The application is referred to a patent examiner for a preliminary examination and search, to ensure that the application complies with the requirements of the Act;

(4) Publication (**s 16(1)** of the **PA 1977**) by the Intellectual Property Office in the *Official Journal (Patents)* allowing public inspection of the claims. Publication of the patent application can give rise to third-party objections to the grant of the patent;

(5) Substantial examination and search within six months after publication, requested by the applicant;

(6) Grant – the comptroller must publish notice in the *Official Journal of Patents* and a Patent Certificate is issued to the patent proprietor;

(7) A monopoly lasting 20 years from the priority date is granted to the patent proprietor.

If Buffy proceeds with her patent application for her new hair-straightening iron, it is highly likely that, with a registered property, she will be in a much stronger position to negotiate a better fee for her invention. Further, she is likely to obtain a greater financial reward from licensing her invention than from selling it outright.

Common Pitfalls ✘

Do not avoid discussing and citing the requirements of the **Patents Act 1977** as a patent is a property right created by statute.

> **Aim Higher** ★
>
> Consider the commercial implications for the inventor if they successfully patent their invention.

QUESTION 49

Critically analyse the pros and cons of relying on the doctrine of confidential information to protect an invention as opposed to applying for a patent.

Answer Plan

This essay question requires a high level of critical analysis and the development of a strategy for good decision-making following analysis of the legal protection afforded by the two regimes. One should not forget, however, to refer to relevant legislation and case law where appropriate.

❖   Nature of patent protection under the **Patents Act 1977**;
❖   Nature of confidential information protection;
❖   How to choose between confidential information and patent protection.

ANSWER

All technology begins with ideas, information and know-how. While the proprietors generally wish to let others know that the new technology is effective, they also want to keep other information confidential in order to secure a patent or other intellectual property right, or because there is no other form of intellectual property right available for that information. For example, certain know-how may not be protected by the claims of a patent specification.

A patent is a legally recognised 20-year monopoly which the government grants in exchange for a complete disclosure of how to make and use an invention: **Patents Act 1977**. Confidential information, on the other hand, covers a wide variety of categories of information such as personal secrets (*Argyll v Argyll* (1967)); commercial records (*Anton Piller KG v Manufacturing Processes Ltd* (1976)); trade secrets (*Seager v Copydex* (1967)); and government secrets (*AG v Guardian Newspapers* (1990)). To be protected, the information must have 'the necessary quality of confidence about it, namely, it must not be something which is public property and public knowledge' (per Lord Greene MR in *Saltman Engineering Co Ltd v Campbell Engineering Co Ltd* (1963)).

Tension frequently exists between the options of keeping an invention confidential or filing a patent application which discloses the invention. Relying on the equitable doctrine of confidential information may eliminate any possibility of ever being able to patent an invention if the secret is later disclosed and enters into the public domain. That said, the publication of a patent destroys any confidential information which it discloses. Sometimes, the choice to patent an invention or to maintain it as confidential information is clear. Usually, however, the decision involves a balancing exercise between the various commercial and legal factors.

Because of the disclosure requirements of patents and the secrecy requirements of confidential information, these two forms of intellectual property cannot usually co-exist for any one particular technology. A choice must be made either to patent the invention or to keep it confidential.

HOW TO CHOOSE BETWEEN CONFIDENTIAL INFORMATION AND PATENT PROTECTION

In deciding whether to proceed with a patent, many factors must be considered. Several factors weigh strongly in favour of patenting. Other factors weigh strongly in favour of maintaining the invention as confidential. Other considerations are less clear in favour of one alternative or the other and require a balancing of several factors.

The critical factor is to assess how realistic it is to keep the information confidential and for how long.

❖ If the information can be kept confidential for approximately as long as the commercial life of the products made using it, patent protection may not be required.
❖ Equally, if the information can be kept confidential for even longer than the 20-year patent term, the information might be best protected as confidential information.

However, the duration of confidential information is uncertain. The protection for the confidential information can be lost overnight if the secret is publicly disclosed, even if the disclosure was not intentional.

THE NEED-TO-KNOW FACTOR AND EX-EMPLOYEES

In relation to a typical business, if only a few people need to know about the invention, secrecy may be a viable option. The difficulty arises when employees leave. The ex-employee may be subject to a contractual restraint of trade obligation, but this is limited in duration and scope. In other words, an ex-employee cannot be restrained from using every 'secret', especially if it is their stock in trade.

REVERSE-ENGINEERING

Another consideration is whether the information can be kept secret after the product has been made available to the public – can the product be easily reverse-engineered? Confidential information does not protect against reverse-engineering, which is lawful unless patent-protected. Accordingly, it is of no use to protect a product which can be reverse-engineered. In this situation, a patent is the only option.

A classic example is the formula for Coca-Cola, which has not to date been reverse-engineered. If the formula had been patented when it was first used in 1886, the formula would have been in the public domain a century ago and would now be free for anyone to use. However, by maintaining the formula as a trade secret, Coca-Cola has continued to dominate the worldwide soft drinks industry.

INDEPENDENT INVENTION

Similarly, the equitable doctrine of confidential information is of little use when dealing with an invention that is likely to be independently invented by another. In fact, this situation presents the dangerous possibility that the second inventor may file for and obtain a patent on the invention. The second inventor may then prevent the proprietor of the confidential information from practising the invention. Therefore, filing a patent application is the clear choice in this situation, especially where the proprietor is in a race with competitors to invent.

MARKET LIFE OF THE PRODUCT

It is important to consider the nature of the invention; a product with a short market life, such as an electronic children's game designed to be updated annually, may be adequately protected by confidential information, giving the proprietor a good 'head start' in the market. However, compare this with an invention for an X-ray airport security system that may become a worldwide standard for many years.

If the major competitive advantage is by being 'first-to-market' or if the technology will be obsolete in less time than it would take for a patent to be issued, then a patent is of little or no use.

THE NEED TO GRANT LICENCES

For the invention to be licensed out, a licensee may be more willing to pay for an invention that is patented. Licensees may worry that their rights are less clearly defined by the doctrine of confidential information and that the value of a licensed invention may be abruptly lost if the licensor fails to maintain the secret.

PATENT APPLICATIONS REMAIN CONFIDENTIAL UNTIL PUBLICATION

The decision to file a patent application is not irrevocable. The act of filing a patent application does not result in loss of confidential information rights. In the United Kingdom, patent applications are kept confidential and are generally published eighteen months after the initial filing date. Therefore, if a patent is not granted on an application, or if the application is abandoned, the confidential information disclosed in the application will not be published and secrecy can be maintained.

Therefore, one effective strategy may be to file a patent application and also to continue to maintain confidential information during the application process. This will provide a substantial delay in the need to decide whether to abandon confidential information status in favour of a patent.

COST

A further advantage of confidential information over patents is that there are no official prosecution costs or maintenance fees in order to establish confidential information or to keep it in force. Patenting costs may amount to several thousand pounds or more. These costs are not incurred if an invention is maintained as confidential information.

However, this does not mean that there are no costs involved in maintaining confidential information. Quite the opposite; in some circumstances, confidential information can be expensive to maintain. For instance, there may be costs associated with physically preventing the public from learning the confidential information. These costs may include: physical plant construction to restrict access to the grounds and buildings; checking on repair and service people; restricting information to individuals in the company who need to know; fragmenting information so that no single individual has access to complete confidential information; labelling containers so that process variables and ingredients are not shown; marking documents as confidential; and using encryption technology. There may also be legal costs for the preparation of contracts which clarify the existence of confidential information and the duty not to disclose. These contracts may have to be signed by suppliers, licensees, customers, consultants and others with whom the proprietor does business, such as those considering engaging in a joint venture, or to include restraint of trade terms for employees leaving the organisation.

The costs and difficulties encountered in maintaining confidential information can be significant to the extent that this consideration is enough to tip the balance in favour of patenting, despite the fact that other considerations might favour relying on the doctrine of confidential information.

FREEDOM OF INFORMATION AND THE PUBLIC INTEREST

Another difficulty with maintaining an invention as confidential may occur whenever documents are submitted to the government. Due to the UK's **Freedom of Information Act 2000**, it can be problematic to prevent information contained in these documents from being discovered by competitors or litigants who make freedom of information requests under the Act. This is because the government can argue that a public interest excuses its use or disclosure of the information.

CONCLUSION

Whether to seek or rely on the doctrine of confidential information is a complex matter that needs to be considered on an individual case basis by examining the specific facts related to the case.

In at least two situations, patents are a clear choice over maintaining an invention as confidential. If an invention can be reverse-engineered or independently developed, if there is a need to disseminate information about the invention, or if the invention is a technology for which a licensee will only pay if it is patented, then the choice is clearly in favour of patents. On the other hand, if the information or know-how is not patentable, if it provides an advantage which is of a shorter duration than the time that it would take to obtain a patent, or if the information will be valuable for a very long time and secrecy can be maintained during that time, then the choice is clearly in favour of confidential information. For the most part, the choice is not black and white, so the various commercial and legal considerations must be carefully weighed up in order to arrive at a reasoned and practical decision.

Common Pitfalls ✗

Avoid stating everything you know about how patents are granted followed by a lengthy discussion of the legal principles in connection with the equitable doctrine of confidential information.

Aim Higher ★

Use headings to add structure to your essay by highlighting the specific issues you are critically analysing. The key here is to carefully analyse the issues that should be taken into account when determining which regime to rely on in order to protect the innovation.

QUESTION 50

There are few legal regimes that are so firmly involved with the promotion of investment and innovation as the laws governing the creation and exploitation of intellectual property. Yet, as a society, we are blissfully unaware of the significance of these laws and take little, if any, time or effort to consider how they might be made to work better . . . [T]he law of intellectual property has a pivotal role in providing both incentive and security for those engaging and investing in the innovative process.

> Sam Ricketson, 'The Future of Australian Intellectual Property Law Reform and Administration' (1992) 3 AIPJ 1 at 3, 5.

▶ Critically discuss.

Answer plan

This question requires a student to consider a quote by a famous intellectual property law academic, and go on to demonstrate a knowledge of the range of intellectual property rights which exist and how they could better serve the interests of society, in particular as a means to encourage investment in new creative endeavours.

- ❖ Explain and define the term 'intellectual property'.
- ❖ Analyse the rationale for granting statutory monopolies and give examples.
- ❖ Consider how the existing regime could 'work better' to promote security and investment in the innovative process and maximise the benefits for society as a whole.

ANSWER

Engaging and investing in the innovative process requires intellectual curiosity, effort and resources. In order to encourage innovation, society has adopted an intellectual property law rights regime. The term 'intellectual property rights' (IPRs) is used to describe the various rights that afford legal protection to innovative and creative endeavour, known in a business sense as 'intangibles'. The rights that fall within the field of intellectual property have developed over time and are now quite wide-ranging and include:

(1) Patents. A patent is a statutory property right governed by the **Patents Act (PA) 1977** that gives the patent owner the exclusive right to use certain inventions.

(2) Copyright. Copyright is a statutory right governed by the **Copyright, Designs and Patents Act (CDPA) 1988** subsisting in original literary, dramatic, musical and artistic works, sound recordings, films, broadcasts, cable programmes and the typography of published editions. Owners of copyright have several economic rights in their works, including the right to prevent unauthorised copyright and adaptations.

(3) Moral rights. Moral rights are statutory rights under the **CDPA 1988** that authors retain in their works, irrespective of who owns the economic rights.

(4) Trade marks. Registered trade marks are statutory rights, as provided by the **Trade Marks Act (TMA) 1994.** This gives the owner the exclusive right to use a distinctive sign (for example a name, symbol, tune, etc.) in relation to a product or service.

(5) Geographical indications (or indications of source or appellations of origin). These are signs assuring consumers that produce comes from, or has been processed in, a particular region renowned for the quality of such produce. Familiar examples include Champagne, Scotch whisky and Parma ham. The UK is bound by **Art 22(2)** of the World Trade Organization's **Agreement on Trade-Related Aspects of Intellectual Property Rights (TRIPS)** to prevent the use of any means in the designation or presentation of a good that indicates or suggests that the good in question originates in a geographical area other than the true place of origin in a manner which misleads the public as to the geographical origin of the good.

(6) Design. A registered design is a statutory right under the **Registered Designs Act (RDA) 1949** that gives the exclusive right to use certain features of the appearance of a range of products. The unregistered design right is the right under the **CDPA 1988** to prevent copying of aspects of the shape or configuration of an article.

The common law and equity also continue to feature in the protection of intellectual property:

(7) Passing off. Goodwill is a form of intangible property consisting of the market's perception of the quality and value of a business and its products, which can be protected by the common law tort of passing off. Passing off is a common law tort or cause of action used to prevent a third party from making misrepresentations which damage the goodwill of another.

(8) Breach of confidence. The equitable doctrine of breach of confidence is used to protect certain confidential information which does not fall within the scope of the other intellectual property law systems set out above, against unauthorised disclosure or use.

Some intellectual property rights come into existence automatically (for example copyright, the design right), while others take effect only upon completion of registration (patents, registered trade marks and designs).

Over the centuries, various rulers of the United Kingdom and its governments have recognised that protecting creative endeavour is crucial to the promotion of innovation and entrepreneurship. Not only does it provide an incentive to engage in the innovation process, it also provides security for investment in innovation. It does so by providing exclusive rights or a monopoly, in some cases for a limited duration. Following the Industrial Revolution, the United Kingdom derived the greater part of its wealth from exports of manufactured goods, and this led to a strengthening of the 'industrial' property law system. There is a correlation between industrialisation and patent protection. The 'industrial property' system has since been transformed into an 'intellectual' property system with advances in technology.

However, the goalposts have moved. The modern industries of the twenty-first century – information technology, biotechnology, pharmaceuticals, communications, education and entertainment – are all knowledge-based, requiring the system to be updated to work better. TV formats, image rights, character merchandising and franchising all have significant commercial value which the traditional intellectual property system is struggling to adequately protect. If the United Kingdom is to successfully participate in the global information economy of the new millennium, the importance of the role of intellectual property in addressing the needs of these modern forms of intangible property will need to be better understood and greater attention accorded to ensuring that the intellectual property laws are indeed effective in promoting innovation. In some cases, new *sui generis* legislation is required to grant statutory rights to promote certainty for the investment community to engage in the innovative process. A pressing intellectual property law issue in recent times is copyright infringement in the digital age.

To this end, recently, in 2010, an independent review of how the intellectual property (IP) framework supports growth and innovation was carried out. The review was chaired by Professor Ian Hargreaves, assisted by a panel of experts who consulted a wide variety of stakeholders. The review panel had a remit to look at barriers the IP system may present, with a particular emphasis on new internet companies. An independent report, entitled *Digital Opportunity: A Review of Intellectual Property and Growth*, was presented to government in May 2011. The review proposes a clear change in the strategic direction of IP policy direction designed to ensure that the UK has an IP framework best suited to supporting innovation and promoting economic growth in the digital age. The review makes ten recommendations designed to ensure that the UK has a more suitable IP framework to meet the needs of the digital economy and the UK's increasingly intangibles intensive economy. Apart from modernising copyright infringement and design laws, in the patent field the unified EU Patent Court gets a significant endorsement, the report stating that the government should 'attach the highest immediate priority' to achieving this aim. Intellectual property law enforcement is also covered and the Review suggests the introduction of 'a small claims track for low monetary value IP claims in the Patents County Court' in order to support rights holders in enforcing their rights.

The extension of intellectual property protection is also occurring at the international level. The seven forms of intellectual property outlined above are included in the **TRIPS Agreement**, which was finalised at the end of the Uruguay Round of world trade negotiations in 1993. The **TRIPS Agreement** draws attention to the fact that the various systems of intellectual property protection developed independently of each other and are not based on any shared underlying principle. There is, however, a common thread running through the intellectual property systems that justifies grouping them together and studying them as a whole. Intellectual property is concerned with protecting applications of ideas and information that are of commercial value. This is reflected in the legal definition of intellectual property, which focuses on the rights or bundles of rights given for the protection of creative output. Most of the intellectual property systems give the creator exclusive rights over the use of his or her creation (for example a painting or invention) for a limited period of time, and delineate conduct for which the right-owner's permission is required.

A central theme running through the entire field of intellectual property is the necessity of striking a balance between the interests of right-owners on the one hand and those of users and the general public on the other. Intellectual property law systems are concerned not only with providing incentives and reward to authors and inventors, but also aim to promote the dissemination and use of new ideas, information and technology for the benefit of society as a whole. If the appropriate balance is struck, the flow of new and innovative ideas will be optimised, whereas protection which is either too broad or inadequate will not be conducive to optimal levels of innovation. The attempt to balance the interests of innovators and the broader community is evident in the exceptions provided in the various intellectual property regimes.

In conclusion, the extension of legal protection to intellectual creations is not without its critics. Arguments against the recognition of intellectual property rights have been made with renewed force in the context of debates about the regulation of the internet, methods of business and biotechnological inventions. The government has a responsibility to its people to adequately consider supplementing the existing intellectual property law systems to deal with modern forms of intangible property in consultation with the relevant stakeholders, and by commissioning reports such as *Digital Opportunity*, the future policy direction of intellectual property laws are being investigated. Accordingly, as stated by Ricketson, 'there are few legal regimes that are so firmly involved with the promotion of investment and innovation as the laws governing the creation and exploitation of intellectual property.' Professor Ricketson would no doubt welcome the United Kingdom's increased awareness of the significance of intellectual property laws and how they might be made to work better to provide both incentive and security for those engaging and investing in the innovative process.

Common Pitfalls ✘

Avoid simply launching into a list of the various intellectual property rights without first setting the context. Set the context for the essay by drafting an introductory paragraph that addresses Sam Ricketson's quote directly.

Aim Higher ★

Provide an up-to-date discussion of the development of the intellectual property law regime by referring to Professor Hargreaves' *Digital Opportunity* report (2011), which supports Professor Ricketson's statement regarding the significance of intellectual property laws and how they might be made better to achieve society's aims.

QUESTION 51

The UK has been successful in its bid to host the 2020 Winter Olympic Games in the Nordic sport and ski resort village of Alston, Cumbria, in northern England. The Government's Department of Culture, Media and Sport has established the Alston Winter Olympics Advisory Committee to draft new legislation (as required by the International Olympics Committee) to protect the intellectual property in the Alston Games and that of its sponsors. Discuss your proposals for such legislation and the nature of the Games' intellectual property needing protection. Critically analyse any other relevant UK legislation that may already offer some form of protection in these circumstances.

Answer plan

This question is very topical, in view of the London 2012 Olympics and the legislative measures recently implemented to protect the Games' intellectual property from ambush marketing.

❖ Consider the nature of the Games' trade marks;
❖ Discuss the relevant provisions of the **Olympic Symbol etc. (Protection) Act 1995**;
❖ Consider s 4(5) of the **Trade Marks Act 1994**;
❖ Analyse the **London Olympic Games and Paralympic Games Act 2006**.

ANSWER

The Alston Winter Olympics Advisory Committee (the Committee) will need to ensure that a legal framework exists to protect the Olympic brand, words, symbols and logos. This is important because raising revenue from the private sector through sponsorship, official merchandise and tickets will largely fund the Games. Official sponsors will expect nothing less than an 'exclusive' association with the Games. They will require contractual assurances that the Committee will protect their interests from competing businesses that will try to engage in 'ambush' marketing by seeking to create an unauthorised association with the Games. If all businesses can create an association with the Games, there is no reason to pay to become an official sponsor. The Committee must take steps to protect the 'Games' brand to ensure unauthorised people are prevented from using the brand without an official sponsorship contract.

TRADE MARKS OF THE GAMES' BRAND

The names, phrases, marks, logos and designs related to the 2020 Alston Winter Olympics and the Olympic and Paralympic Movements (collectively known as the Games' marks) should be made official trade marks, owned or licensed by the 2020 Alston Winter Olympics Committee. Examples of the Games' marks are set out below:

❖ The Olympic symbol;
❖ The Paralympic symbol;
❖ The words 'Paralympic', 'Paralympiad', 'Paralympian' (and their plurals);
❖ The Paralympic motto, 'Spirit in Motion';
❖ The Olympic motto, '*Citius Altius Fortius*' and its translation, 'Faster Higher Stronger';
❖ The words 'Olympic', 'Olympiad', 'Olympian' (and their plurals);

❖ The Paralympics Great Britain (GB) logo;
❖ The Team Great Britain (GB) logo;
❖ The British Olympic Association logo.

New marks to be protected in connection with the 2020 Alston Winter Olympics will include, for example, the Alston 2020 logo and the words 'Alston 2020' and 'Alston 2020.com' (and various derivatives).

HOW CAN THE COMMITTEE PROTECT THE GAMES' MARKS?

The Games' marks are legally protected by a variety of means. Trade mark law protects some of the above items and others attract copyright protection. Special laws have been enacted in the UK to give extra protection to some of the Games' marks.

The **Olympic Symbol etc. (Protection) Act 1995 (OSPA 1995)** protects the Olympic and Paralympic symbols, mottos and various words. In addition, **s 4(5)** of the **Trade Marks Act 1994** provides further protection by giving the Trade Marks Registrar the power to refuse to register a mark that consists of a controlled representation trade mark within the meaning of **OSPA 1995**, unless of course the trade mark application is made by a person appointed under the Act.

It would be advisable for the Alston 2020 Committee to consider drafting new legislation entitled, for example, the 'Alston Olympic Games and Paralympic Games Act', so as to obtain extra protection for the brand. This proposed new legislation would probably be based on the provision of the recent **London Olympic Games and Paralympic Games Act 2006** (the '**2006 Act**').

WHAT IS NOT PERMITTED UNDER THE 2006 ACT?

The unauthorised use of any of the Games' marks, or any other marks or logos that are confusingly similar to, or likely to be mistaken for them, is strictly prohibited. For example, it would be unlawful to use the Olympic symbol or the London 2012 logo or mark in the course of trade without a licence (permission) from the Organising Committee. These aspects of the Games' brand cannot be used on goods, in business names, on business papers or in advertising without written permission.

THE NEW 'ASSOCIATION RIGHT'

The **2006 Act** created what is known as a new 'association right'. In other words, only exclusive sponsors have the right to be exclusively associated with the Games. It is an offence to falsely represent any association, affiliation, endorsement, sponsorship or similar relationship with London 2012, the British Olympic and Paralympic teams or any other part of the Olympic Movement. It is through the new 'association right' that the 2006 Act attempts to deal with the problem of ambush marketing in order to protect its sponsors.

WHO IS ALLOWED TO USE THE GAMES' BRAND?

Only official sponsors, suppliers and licensees will be allowed to use the Games' marks in line with the terms and conditions of their sponsorship agreements with the 2020 Alston Advisory Committee or the International Olympic Committee. A statutory register of official sponsors will be created and only those listed on the register can use the Games' brand.

WHAT IF SOMEONE USES THE GAMES' BRAND WITHOUT A LICENCE?

Under the **OSPA 1995**, any unauthorised use of the Games' brand is an offence. Similar provisions should be included in any proposed new Alston 2020 Games legislation. If necessary, however, the Alston 2020 Advisory Committee should be prepared to enforce its ownership of the Games' brand in the interest of reassuring and protecting its sponsors' interests. Remedies that a court could award to protect the Games' brand might include orders to seize unauthorised merchandise and pay damages.

Common Pitfalls ✗

Avoid a journalistic style discussing only ambush marketing and examples of ambush marketing from previous Olympic Games. Focus on how the new Act now protects the Games' intellectual property.

Aim Higher ★

Aim to discuss enforcement of the provisions of the new Act as well as any criticism from stakeholders regarding those provisions.

QUESTION 52

Confidential information is said to be a very 'risky' form of intellectual property. Why is this and how can a business prevent the disclosure of its confidential information?

Answer Plan

- Discuss the nature of confidential information in contrast to other forms of intellectual property.
- Define the doctrine of confidential information and the elements of a course of action for breach of the doctrine.
- Consider the use of nondisclosure agreements, their purpose and contents.

ANSWER

Confidential information is not like patents, copyright or designs, where a particular 'thing' is afforded protection. Rather, know-how or certain information is valuable precisely because it is secret and not in the public domain, available for everyone to use. There is no system of registration, nor any registered right to access.

Exactly what the confidential information actually is can be difficult to establish with certainty. Does it include information contained in correspondence, research reports, customer lists, emails or even conversations?

The doctrine of confidential information is a set of legal principles, developed to allow a great degree of flexibility because English law does not distinguish between types of information that may be protected. The fundamental principle is that a person who has received confidential information from another will not take unfair advantage of it or profit from the wrongful use or publication of it. The range of information that can be protected is wide and may include trade or technological secrets and know-how, commercial goods or recipes (the Coca-Cola recipe is still a secret!).

In the UK, if confidential information is unlawfully disclosed the proprietor of the confidential information may bring a legal action for 'breach of confidence' in court. The case of *Coco v AN Clark (Engineers) Ltd* (1969) established the three elements of the action as follows. The information:

(1) must have a necessary element of confidentiality, that is, not be in the public domain, nor information that is public property;
(2) was communicated under an obligation to keep it confidential; and
(3) is used in an unauthorised way, possibly to the detriment of the party communicating it.

A nondisclosure agreement (an 'NDA', or confidentiality agreement as they are commonly called) requires the signatory to swear that they will keep the information disclosed to them (ideas, trade secrets and other non-public information) confidential.

A nondisclosure agreement has two main purposes:

(1) Practically, in order to prevent misunderstanding, to inform the recipient that the information being disclosed is confidential; and
(2) Legally, to have written evidence that will assist in proving elements of the potential claimant's case.

NDAs have traditionally been used among lawyers, investment bankers and others involved in large corporate deals. However, they are also gaining currency among entrepreneurs and inventors, particularly those in the high-tech industries. An NDA is legally enforceable as a contract and in equity, so if the recipient breaches the agreement and releases the confidential information to a third party or to the public, the disclosing party can sue for damages or an account of profits as well as seek an injunction to stop further disclosure. The founder of Hotmail, Sabeer Bhatia, amassed over 400 NDAs in the years leading up to the sale of his company to Microsoft for approximately £200 million.

While the use of NDAs in business is increasingly common, some people and businesses are reluctant to sign them because they believe the obligation to keep the confidence is too onerous. It is hard to keep secrets, especially over lots of information for years and, particularly, to ensure that company employees will keep those secrets too. This will necessitate internal policies and procedures, as well as keeping track of ex-employees who leave the business. Venture capitalists, securities analysts and successful technology companies in particular are often reluctant to sign NDAs, because they see too many similar ideas and do not want to be obligated in respect of one over another. Nevertheless, if carefully drafted to ensure the obligation of confidentiality has sensible limits, NDAs will continue to flourish. Remember, if information is not protected:

❖ as confidential information; or
❖ by some other form of intellectual property right, for example, copyright, patent law, etc.

anyone else is free to use it and disclose it.

Finally, note that as the doctrine of confidential information is an Anglo-American law concept, the general law obligations of confidence may not be protected in other countries. Some countries (e.g. Latin American countries) may even have laws that prevent the creation of obligations of confidence.

Common Pitfalls ✘

This essay question expects the student to demonstrate a solid understanding of the law, namely the equitable doctrine of confidential information. There is no legislation to discuss here.

Aim Higher ★

Evaluate the practical steps that an enterprise can take to prevent the disclosure of confidential information and trade secrets.

QUESTION 53

Write a short answer explaining the meaning and legal protection provided by each of the following terms:

(1) Protected designation of origin;
(2) Protected geographical indication of origin;
(3) Certificate of special character.

Answer Plan

This is a typical subdivided short answer question on the subject of geographical indications. Answer each sub-question in turn, clearly identifying the separate parts (1) to (3) in numerical order. Assume that each subdivision carries equal marks unless told otherwise.

❖ Note that the common factor with all the terms is that they are indications of source, provenance or origin.
❖ Discuss the concept of a 'geographical indication' as a form of intellectual property.
❖ Note Articles 22–24 of the Trade Related Agreement on Intellectual Property (TRIPS).

ANSWER

With the increased mobility of goods since the Industrial Revolution and now globalisation, there is an increased potential for confusion as to the origin of goods, including the deliberate free-riding on the reputation of the products that emanate from a particular place. An indication of source is simply an indication of provenance or origin; examples include French perfume, Italian wine and German cars. However, there are legal protections for more specific and valuable associations between a product and the region from which it originates, as discussed below. These amount to property rights within the field of intellectual property.

(1)   PROTECTED DESIGNATION OF ORIGIN

Legal protection is available for geographical terms when a valuable association has been created over time between a product and the region from which it originates, such as 'Champagne' or 'Orkney beef'. Producers or traders from the region sharing the name may apply for either UK domestic legal protection or European Community rights. In the EU, this right is called a 'protected designation of origin' (PDO). A PDO is a sign used on goods stating that a given product originates in a given geographical area and possesses qualities or a reputation due to that place of origin. A PDO product must originate from the particular area, be fully produced, processed and prepared in that area and have qualities and characteristics that are exclusive due to the geographical area's local environment. Only groups of producers may apply for a PDO to be registered. Accordingly, it is a form of 'collective' intellectual property right. A PDO designation affords the highest level of protection for geographical indications.

(2)   PROTECTED GEOGRAPHICAL INDICATION OF ORIGIN

The criteria for a protected geographical indication (GI) are less stringent than for a PDO. However, GIs are also registered under the EU **PDO Regulation**. The difference between a PDO and a GI is that for a GI the geographical link must arise *in at least one* of the stages of production, processing or preparation (**Art 2(1)** of the **PDO Regulation**). GIs may be used for a variety of products, particularly agricultural products. A number of GIs have been registered in the UK, for example Rutland Bitter, Exmoor Blue Cheese, Welsh Lamb and many more.

(3)   CERTIFICATE OF SPECIAL CHARACTER (CSC)

This is the term given to traditional foods and recipes registered under the **1992 EU Regulation** on certificates of special character for agricultural products and foodstuffs, known as **'The Traditional Foods Regulation'**. Specific character is defined to mean the 'features or set of features which distinguishes an agricultural product or a foodstuff clearly from other similar products or foodstuffs belonging to the same category'. To be granted CSC status, the name to be registered must: (1) be specific; (2) express the specific character of the foodstuff or product; (3) be traditional or established by custom (**Art 2(1)**). As well as granting property rights over the use of the registered CSC name, registration also authorises producers to use the words 'Traditional Speciality Guaranteed' and the accompanying logo.

Usually, the grant of PDO, GI or CSC status enables the producer to charge more for their goods because of their unique and sometimes superior qualities and exclusivity. These products have acquired a valuable reputation and if not legally protected are vulnerable to be misrepresented by dishonest commercial operators. False use of GIs leads to two key consequences. First, valuable business is lost and consumers are deceived, and second, the established reputation of the products is diluted.

In conclusion, GIs as a general concept are understood by consumers to denote the origin and quality of products. Many of them have acquired valuable reputations which, if not adequately protected, may be misrepresented by dishonest commercial operators. False use of geographical indications by unauthorised parties is detrimental to consumers and legitimate producers. The former are deceived and led into believing they are buying a genuine product with specific qualities and characteristics, while they usually in fact get a cheaper imitation. The latter suffer damage because valuable business is lost and the established reputation of their products is damaged.

Common Pitfalls ✗

It is tempting to illustrate your answer by providing many examples of famous products that you may have heard of; however, it is more important to discuss the legal authority for the different forms of geographical indication protection.

Aim Higher ★

Following your answers to (1) to (3), add value by making some thoughtful concluding remarks which depict the need for such a regime.

Appendix I
Exam Question Methodology

Business law exams commonly contain four types of questions: essay, problem, short answer and multiple choice. An assessment is usually pedagogically designed to give the student the opportunity to display the following skills:

i. Evaluation;
ii. Synthesis;
iii. Analysis;
iv. Application;
v. Comprehension;
vi. Knowledge.

PREPARING FOR THE EXAM

❖ Study alone first, carefully reviewing your course notes. Once you feel more confident, study with classmates.
❖ Take turns asking each other questions. This type of practice will expose gaps in your knowledge. Group time should be used for practice, not for review and discussion.
❖ Simulate what you will be asked to do in the exam. For example, if you are sitting a closed-book business law exam, it is important that you practise answering different business law questions from this volume of *Q&A Business Law* without access to your notes or textbook.
❖ Practise regularly rather than cram in one long session.
❖ Don't psych yourself out!
❖ Carrying extra emotional baggage, for example, 'I don't want to fail, I just want to pass!' can lead to your performance flagging.
❖ Arrange to see the tutor/lecturer if you need extra help with techniques or advice well BEFORE the exam.

DURING THE EXAM

❖ Read through the exam questions a couple of times very carefully. Don't panic or read too hurriedly.

❖ Choose which questions you will answer and allocate an amount of time to spend answering each question.

❖ Try to work out which skills the question requires and make sure that you demonstrate those skills.

❖ Underline or highlight important words or phrases.

❖ Identify the legal issues that the question raises.

❖ Make short notes in the margin about ideas, cases and legal principles that seem relevant.

❖ Confirm exactly what the question asks you to do – discuss, advise, analyse …

❖ Apply the relevant legislation and case law to the issues and reach a conclusion.

❖ Whenever you can, use cases and legislation as authority for statements of law. However, there is no need to repeat the detailed facts of every case as this is a waste of time. Try to summarise the facts of the case in a sentence or two in order to demonstrate the similarity of the case to the facts at hand.

TYPES OF BUSINESS LAW ASSESSMENTS

ESSAY QUESTIONS

An essay question is often a short statement of law contained in a quote from a court judgment or an academic article, which requires the student to answer the query or proposition within it. Essay questions are designed to test the student's depth of understanding of business law and issues as well as their ability to critically analyse the law. The best approach is to adopt a succinct style following an answer plan that covers the basic principles. Three examples of typical essay question terminology are set out below:

'CRITICALLY ANALYSE'

You may be asked to 'critically analyse … .'. In this case, a useful approach is to provide an objective assessment of the positive and negative points of the subject. Ensure that your answer is clearly structured to signpost the progression of your argument(s).

'DISCUSS'

Another commonly used instructing word is 'discuss'. This is an instruction to discuss the key words identified in the essay question.

SUBDIVIDED QUESTIONS

Some essay questions are broken down into subsections, for example (i), (ii) . . . or (a), (b) . . . etc. The best approach to this type of question is to answer each sub-question in turn, clearly identifying the separate parts of the essay. Unless you are told otherwise, it is reasonable for you to assume that each subdivision carries equal marks. This means you may want to allocate equal time to each subsection.

ESSAY QUESTIONS – APPROACH

In general, when dealing with an essay question, the following approach is suggested:

STEP 1

What is the widest possible classification of the specific topic (e.g. contract law, company law, etc.)?

STEP 2

Identify the focus within that topic – for example, whether the principle of limited liability established in the case of *Salomon v Salomon & Co Ltd* [1897] (House of Lords) provides the public with sufficient protection when a company becomes insolvent.

Subject	Company law
Sources of law	**Companies Act 2006**
	Salomon v Salomon & Co Ltd [1897] HL
Topic	Consequences of limited liability
Focus	Whether the public are sufficiently protected in the event of insolvency

STEP 3

Identify the key words in the title and explain and define them in the course of your essay. Refer to relevant statutes and case law that support your thesis. There is no excuse for not citing cases accurately. Use the correct name for an Act (the short title).

STEP 4

❖ Plan your essay with a simple outline. Does the order of the points you have written make sense?

- Use headings to signpost the content of your essay to the marker.
- Include an introductory paragraph that defines key terms and forecasts the structure of the essay. Write using several paragraphs, not just one long paragraph. Each paragraph should cover a distinct aspect of the topic.
- Use concrete examples of case law to support your points along the way.
- Attempt to weave analysis, constructive criticism and evaluation of the law into your essay. There are always two sides to an issue and it is important to engage in a balanced discussion.
- Have a concluding paragraph to summarise your key points and resolve the questions asked.

STEP 5

Review and proofread your essay to ensure that everything mentioned in it is relevant to the title. This is how to attract marks. End your essay with a brief summary and reach a sensible and reasoned conclusion.

If you run out of time, quickly outline the points you had planned to make. This will not get you full marks, but you may get a few additional marks.

PROBLEM QUESTIONS

Problem-solving questions contain a set of hypothetical facts and read like a short story. The facts may be based on or similar to a decided case or may be completely made up. The difficulty lies in recognising the areas of law from the factual circumstances. In answering the problem question, in essence, you put yourself in the position of the judge. Judges try to evaluate the strength of each party's position and arrive at a logically reasoned decision through the application of the relevant law. A problem question is NOT an invitation to write an essay. The facts of the case are important and should be specifically referred to in your answer. Most business law problem questions can be dealt with by adopting the following methodology:

BUSINESS LAW PROBLEM QUESTION CHECKLIST

- Classify the key facts (e.g. items of property, relevant dates, significant events, etc.).
- Identify the area(s) of business law concerned.
- Identify the parties.
- Note all the elements that need to be proved.
- Explain the applicable law and conclude as you progress.
- Consider any supporting arguments or whether any defences apply.
- If the cause of action is established, consider what remedies are available.
- Advise the parties as to the strength of their case.

Examiners differ in their preferred practice for answering problem questions. The above checklist is general guidance. There are also two acronyms that may help when dealing with problem questions:

IRAC	Issues	IDEA	Identify the legal issue
	Rules		**D**efine the legal rule
	Apply		**E**xplain how the rule works
	Conclude		**A**pply the rule to the facts

SHORT-ANSWER QUESTIONS

Short-answer questions are often open-ended questions that require students to create an answer. Short-answer items typically require responses of one word to a few sentences. 'Fill in the blank' and 'completion' questions are examples of short-answer question types.

The point of short-answer questions is to test your retention of information and, compared with essay questions, they are relatively easier to write.

Read the questions CAREFULLY! Ask yourself, what are they specifically asking? Try to write a specific, clear explanation. Do this by:

❖ Getting to the point; don't rewrite the question.
❖ Using an example; make sure it is clear why you are using that example to answer the question.
❖ Writing a concise answer; an answer that's longer than necessary will not cause you to lose points, as long as everything you write is correct. But if your extra statements are *incorrect*, you will probably LOSE marks. In addition, writing more than necessary *wastes time* that could be spent on other questions. So you should only write more if you think it is more likely to gain you points (because it is correct *and* crucial to answering the question) than to lose you points (because it is incorrect).

There are four basic types of short-answer question:

DEFINITION QUESTIONS

For these questions, you simply need to define a concept.

❖ Example: 'Define the concept of "legal capacity" in the context of contract law.'

EXPLANATION QUESTIONS

For these questions, you need to explain *why* something is true or *how* something works.

❖ Example: 'Explain the doctrine of *stare decisis*.'

EXAMPLE QUESTIONS

For these questions, you need to state one or more *specific*, real-world instances of some concept.

❖ Example: 'List three cases that illustrate the issue of discrimination in employment law.'

RELATIONSHIP QUESTIONS

For these questions, you need to state how two or more things relate to each other. Are they opposites? Are they the same thing? Is one an example of the other? How do they differ? and so forth. These are usually the most difficult questions.

❖ Example: 'What is the relationship between a limited liability company and its directors?'

Remember, it is always better to write something than nothing at all. Do not leave blank spaces. If it is a definition question but all you can think of is an example, then give the example. If it is an explanation question but all you can think of is the definition, then give the definition. You will not get full credit, but you *might* get partial credit.

MULTIPLE-CHOICE QUESTIONS

The following tips are helpful for answering multiple-choice questions.

❖ Use the process of elimination: cross out answers you know are incorrect, and then focus on the remaining answers.
❖ Look for the *best* answer to the question, not just any answer that seems correct.
❖ Pay special attention to words like *not, sometimes, always* and *never*. Responses that use absolute words such as 'always' or 'never' are less likely to be correct than ones that use conditional words like 'usually' or 'probably'.
❖ Don't waste too much time on a question you are having problems with. Move on and go back to it later if you have time.

❖ It is better to guess than not to answer the question at all (unless you are penalised for giving incorrect answers – check!).

❖ If all else fails, choose response (b) or (c). Many lecturers subconsciously feel that the correct answer is 'hidden' better if it is surrounded by distractors. Response (a) is usually least likely to be the correct one.

GRAMMAR, SYNTAX AND SPELLING

Developing a good writing style is crucial for law students because the law is all about communicating through words. Keep sentences relatively short to avoid grammar and syntax errors. Do not adopt an overly journalistic or casual style of writing. On the other hand, avoid grandiose and flowery language. Use plain English where possible and write succinctly. Well-written answers have more authority and will attract better marks.

From your experience of exams so far, you know that beginning to write is difficult, so do not start writing until you have an idea of what you want to say. Creating a brief answer outline will help you to plan the beginning, middle and end of your answer.

LOST FOR WORDS?

Legal writing requires quite formal language and style. Set out in the table below are some words and phrases to help you.

Sequencing	Referencing	Showing contrast	Concluding
First	According to . . .	Nevertheless	Therefore
To begin with	. . . define	However	In conclusion
In addition	. . . suggests that	Conversely	To summarise
Moreover	. . . states	Although	In brief
Another	. . . maintains that	Whereas	Thus
Furthermore	. . . outlines	Notwithstanding	Finally
Subsequently	. . . focuses on	Despite this	To sum up
Consequently	. . . argues	Alternately	Overall

Appendix II
Useful Websites

ALTERNATIVE DISPUTE RESOLUTION
British and Irish Ombudsman Association: www.bioa.org.uk
Civil Justice Council: www.adr.civiljusticecouncil.gov.uk
Community Legal Service: www.legalservices.gov.uk/civil.asp

CIVIL JUSTICE
Civil Justice Council: www.civiljusticecouncil.gov.uk
Civil Law Policy: www.justice.gov.uk

COMPANY LAW
Companies House: www.companieshouse.gov.uk

CONSUMER LAW
Office of Fair Trading: www.oft.gov.uk

COURTS AND TRIBUNALS
Auld Committee Review of Criminal Courts: www.criminal-courts-review.org.uk
Courts services and judgments: www.justice.gov.uk
Criminal Justice System: www.justice.gov.uk

ENGLISH LAW AND LEGAL RESOURCES
Gateway to a variety of legal resources: www.venables.co.uk
Legislation.gov.uk: www.legislation.gov.uk/
Legal abbreviations: www.legalabbrevs.cardiff.ac.uk
Legal information: www.infolaw.co.uk

EQUAL OPPORTUNITIES
Equality and Human Rights Commission: www.equalityhumanrights.com/

EUROPEAN COMMUNITY LAW

European Commission: http://ec.europa.eu/index_en.htm

European Council: www.consilium.europa.eu

European Court of Justice: http://europa.eu/about-eu/institutions-bodies/court-justice/index_en.htm

European Union: http://europa.eu

Future of the European Union: http://ec.europa.eu/public_opinion/archives/ebs/ebs_251_en.pdf

HUMAN RIGHTS

Human Rights Unit, Ministry of Justice: http://webarchive.nationalarchives.gov.uk/+/http://www.justice.gov.uk/about/human-rights.htm

INFORMATION LAW

Society for Computers and Law: www.scl.org

INTELLECTUAL PROPERTY LAW

ACID Anti Copying in Design: http://acid.eu.com

Alliance Against IP Theft: www.allianceagainstiptheft.co.uk

Brand Enforcement: www.brandenforcement.co.uk

Chartered Institute of Patent Attorneys: www.cipa.org.uk

Community Trade Mark/Design Office: http://oami.europa.eu/ows/rw/pages/index.en.do

Copyright Licensing Agency: www.cla.co.uk

Department of Business, Innovation and Skills: www.bis.gov.uk

DBIS, Government Office for Science: www.bis.gov.uk/science

Federation against Copyright Theft: www.fact-uk.org.uk

Federation against Software Theft: www.fast.org.uk

Institute of Patentees and Inventors: www.invent.org.uk

Institute of Trade Mark Attorneys: www.itma.org.uk

Intellectual Property Institute: www.intellectualpropertyinstitute.org

Intellectual Property Owners Association: www.ipo.org

IP Bar Association: www.ipba.co.uk

IP Law Firms Database: www.intellectualpropertylawfirms.com

UK Intellectual Property Office: www.ipo.gov.uk/

United States Patent and Trade Mark Office: www.uspto.org

World Intellectual Property Organization: www.wipo.org

World Trade Organization: www.wto.org

LAW-MAKING

Civil Justice Council: www.judiciary.gov.uk/about-the-judiciary/advisory-bodies/cjc
Houses of Parliament: www.parliament.uk
Justice: www.justice.gov.uk
Law Commission: www.justice.gov.uk/lawcommission/index.htm
UK Acts of Parliament: www.legislation.gov.uk
UK public-sector information: www.direct.gov.uk

LEGAL FORMS OF BUSINESS

British Chamber of Commerce: www.britishchambers.org.uk
British Venture Capital Association: www.bvca.co.uk
Business advice: www.businesslink.org
Companies House: www.companies-house.gov.uk
Federation of Small Businesses: www.fsb.org.uk
HM Revenue and Customs: www.hmrc.gov.uk
Institute of Directors: www.iod.com
The Prince's Trust: www.princes-trust.org.uk

LEGAL PROFESSION

Bar Council (Barristers): www.barcouncil.org.uk
Government Legal Officers: www.justice.gov.uk
Institute of Legal Executives: www.ilex.org.uk
Law Society (Solicitors): www.lawsociety.org.uk
The Judiciary of England and Wales: www.judiciary.gov.uk
The Magistrates' Association: www.magistrates-association.org.uk
Society of Licensed Conveyancers: www.conveyancers.org.uk

Index